10 SIMPLE SECRETS OF THE WORLD'S GREATEST BUSINESS COMMUNICATORS

★ ★ ★

CARMINE GALLO

EMMY AWARD-WINNING
TELEVISION JOURNALIST
AND COMMUNICATIONS COACH

SOURCEBOOKS, INC.®
NAPERVILLE, ILLINOIS

Published by Sourcebooks, Inc.
P.O. Box 4410, Naperville, Illinois   60567-4410
(630) 961-3900
FAX: (630) 961-2168
www.sourcebooks.com

The Library of Congress has cataloged the hardcover edition of this title
as follows:
Gallo, Carmine.
  10 simple secrets of the world's greatest business communicators /
Carmine Gallo.
      p. cm.
  Includes index.
(alk. paper)
  1. Business communication. 2. Communication in management. 3.
Leadership. I. Title: Ten simple secrets of the world's greatest business
communicators. II. Title.

HF5718.G35 2005
658.4'5--dc22

2004029621

Printed and bound in the United States of America
VP 10 9 8 7 6 5 4 3 2 1

To Vanessa for her unwavering support, relentless optimism, and belief in our guiding light.

CONTENTS

INTRODUCTION

YOUR STORY. MY PASSION.

"When you change the way you see yourself as a speaker,
the speaker your audience sees will change."

CARMINE GALLO

You have an extraordinary story to tell. But whether you're pitching a service, product, company, or cause, how you craft and deliver your message makes all the difference. Some people tell their stories better than others—capturing the hearts and minds of everyone in their personal and professional lives. They are considered the world's greatest business communicators—the most electrifying speakers in the corporate world. But while they represent a wide variety of titles, industries, and backgrounds, they share 10 Simple Secrets which have turned them into dazzling presenters. In the pages to follow, you'll hear directly from the world's top contemporary business leaders, many of whom reveal their communication secrets for the first time.

The 10 Simple Secrets will change your life as they have the lives of the communicators who formed the principles. By identifying and adopting the techniques of the world's greatest business communicators, you will:

- Stand apart from your competition
- Generate more leads
- Close more sales
- Raise your visibility
- Advance your business agenda

- Inspire and electrify your audiences
- Potentially change the world with your service, product, company, or cause

Those are some bold promises. But I believe it can happen, given my experience with hundreds of people in my workshops and seminars who discover the secrets for themselves. Their transformations are astonishing—I've seen spokespeople go from dull to dazzling in less than less two hours, simply by adopting the powerful techniques in this book. Think about it. Much of your success is measured by your leadership presence—how you talk, walk, and look. The communicators in this book have it nailed. And so will you.

Consider just a few of the leaders who will share their secrets with you: A man who took his passion for coffee and literally transformed the American landscape, an entrepreneur who reinvented the way millions of people manage their financial lives, and a young woman who leveraged a $1,000 loan to build a billion dollar real estate empire in New York City. They go by rather common names like Howard, Scott, and Barbara. But the companies they built are extraordinary, with names like Starbucks, Intuit, and the Corcoran Group.

Others have ordinary beginnings but enjoy astounding success. You'll hear from Suze Orman, a woman who started as a financial advisor in a small California town and became one of the best-selling authors of our time. We'll talk to a sensational speaker and entrepreneur, Jeff Taylor, who started a simple jobs board on the Internet and literally created a "Monster." You'll learn how a leader with humble beginnings and an unusual name—Schwarzenegger—sharpened his presentation skills to become one of the most powerful and charismatic leaders in the world.

There are many, many more. You'll learn about the presentation and speaking techniques of world famous corporate and political leaders and how you can incorporate their traits in your own professional business communications: You'll read about entrepreneurs like Virgin CEO Richard Branson, political leaders like British prime minister Tony Blair and Nelson Mandela, and world-renowned literary figures like Maya Angelou. You'll read interviews with leading CEOs, executives, entrepreneurs, venture capitalists, experts, professors, and authors. For the first time, they share presentation secrets that have catapulted them to the top of their fields. Make no mistake—they all credit their communication skills for much of their success. Here's a sample of what they told me during dozens of personal interviews:

- "I've been blessed with the ability to communicate with all kinds of people to build a common thread of understanding."—*Howard Schultz, Starbucks chairman*
- "Communication is the most important skill any person in a leadership position could have."—*James Citrin, Global practice leader, Spencer Stuart and author,* The 5 Patterns of Extraordinary Careers
- "Communication is responsible for 90 percent of my success, without a doubt."—*Barbara Corcoran, Founder, The Corcoran Group and author,* Use What You've Got
- "When pitching a product, the spokesperson is at the center of the experience."—*Geoffrey Moore, Author,* Crossing the Chasm
- "I've always felt that as the CEO of an organization, you've got to be willing to put yourself in front of the brand."—*Jeff Taylor, Founder, Monster*
- "I am blessed with the gift of communication and unlimited passion for this topic."—*Suze Orman, CNBC host and personal finance author*
- "I've been in the venture capital business for twenty-five years. I see ten presentations a week. The majority are boring. The spokesperson, who is at the center of the presentation, has to keep me engaged." —*Martin Gagen, Former executive director of 3i Venture Capital*
- "Communication is a very important part of my job, even among the investment community. They won't invest in your stock unless they get a good feel for you as a person."—*John Chen, CEO of Sybase*
- "It's important to communicate a bold vision."—*Scott Cook, Cofounder of Intuit*

Cook and many other high profile CEOs have hired communications coaches to help prepare them for mission critical presentations and speaking appearances. You don't have to. Consider this book your personal communications "coach" complete with stories, interviews, techniques, tips, advice, coaching drills, and Internet links so you can watch master presenters in addition to reading about them. You're holding a bargain when you think about the fact that, combined, the corporate leaders who will share their presentation secrets run companies valued at more than one-quarter of a trillion dollars, manage half a million employees, and have substantial personal wealth—several have a net worth topping a billion dollars.

★ ★ ★

During the 2004 campaign for U.S. President, the little-known former Vermont governor Howard Dean took an early lead in the Democratic Primary. For a few weeks, his campaign broke all sorts of records for fundraising, especially for soliciting money and support over the Internet. Dean was on the cover of *Time* and *Newsweek* simultaneously in one week. But he was clearly uncomfortable and awkward during television interviews—a critical medium to reach voters. After his campaign had sputtered, Dean was interviewed for the Associated Press and asked what he thought he could have done better. "I needed some serious media training," Dean admitted. "I did it on the job but could have saved myself a lot of hassle if I had done it earlier." Anyone who has to persuade or motivate audiences should have a communications coach. Some understand the need early on, while others realize it after it's too late and the damage has been done. This book has more communications coaching advice than you're likely to get from most other resources. I'm grateful that so many dynamic communicators have shared their insights with me. In turn, now I can help you leverage these techniques to improve your own speaking style!

Lincoln Never Used PowerPoint

This book is vastly different from any public speaking or business communications guide on the market today. For starters, you will find no references to Lincoln, Churchill, or Roosevelt—other than now! They are irrelevant to your business presentations. Yet most books in this category continue to pay homage to these historical figures as though you'll miss something critical if the author fails to reference them. Those authors should stop reading now and skip to chapter 10, "Reinvent Yourself." As for the rest of you, keep going, we're just getting started!

Before you take what I say out of context, please understand that I'm a history buff and a student of leadership. But not once in my fifteen years of interviewing the world's top executives did I think for a moment that any of them could improve their presentation skills from a discussion of Lincoln, Churchill, or FDR.

I'd argue that it's unlikely Lincoln, Churchill, or FDR, using the methods they used in their times, could have reached their positions of leadership in contemporary society. They would have had to adapt their presentation styles to connect with modern audiences accustomed to PowerPoint, MTV, and twenty-four-hour cable news. The 10 Simple Secrets are meant for contemporary communicators who need to win over twenty-first century business audiences—listeners who demand passion, clarity, brevity, and authenticity—all wrapped in a visually appealing package.

Here's another problem with using historic leaders as examples of great speakers: I've read that Lincoln was a better writer than speaker. Is that true? I don't know. I've never seen Lincoln—that's the point. You can go to the Internet right now to watch video clips of charismatic and effective leaders who live the 10 Simple Secrets today. You can read about them in newspapers and magazines. You can watch their interviews on television and watch some of them in person at major conferences and conventions. They could be managing your company, your division, your office. It's time to open our eyes to the fabulous business speakers who are among today's greatest leaders.

Believe it or not, there have been one or two great presentations since the Gettysburg Address. Do you know a public speaking book exists in which the author—an actor—tells you how he would read the Gettysburg Address? What exactly are we supposed to learn from that? Now tell me what Lincoln would do with PowerPoint and I'll pay for that! Other than the fact that his big hat would block the slides, who really knows how Lincoln would have presented a PowerPoint show? Who cares? You should be more intrigued by how Starbucks chairman Howard Schultz dazzles his audiences, impresses investors, and inspires employees. Schultz is among dozens of world-class leaders who reveal their secrets in this book. Lincoln wasn't available for interviews.

> ★ ★ ★
>
> Let's face it, even an amazing speaker like John F. Kennedy offers little value for your next presentation. I guarantee that if you end your next staff meeting with these words, it'll be your last: "Let the word go forth to corporate friend and foe alike, that we will pay any price, bear any burden, to ensure the continued profitability and market share growth of our division!"

At this point, somebody who has never had success pitching, promoting, or presenting a service, product, company, or cause will take offense to what I've written and put down the book to send me a nasty email. Before you do, I have another suggestion. Visit Amazon.com, look up any of the twelve thousand six hundred titles on Winston Churchill and spend the next few decades of your life reading some of them. You will be no more successful as a presenter, but it will save me the time of reading your note.

The Single Dumbest Piece of Advice You'll Ever Hear

There are plenty of misconceptions on the topic of communications. One current recommendation perpetuates the dumbest piece of public speaking advice—the single piece of advice that can ruin your career and destroy your personal brand in less than a minute—start by telling a joke. For the majority of presenters, it's a stupid thing to do and it could lead to career suicide. News flash—you're not Chris Rock or Billy Crystal. None of the great communicators profiled in this book kick off their presentations with a joke. Well, New York's real estate queen Barbara Corcoran once did but she tells us why she'll never make that mistake again.

> ★ ★ ★
>
> Beginning your presentation with a humorous aside, observation, or casual reference is different than starting with a joke. The former is meant to elicit a warm smile from your listeners. The moment you kick off your talk with "two people walk into a bar…" you're dead.

The problem lies with the "communications experts" who dispense this advice. Most are no more qualified to teach presentation skills than I am to fly the space shuttle. They're either out-of-work PR types, former college radio DJs, or speaking-competition winners who have a deep affection for the sound of their own voices. Few of them have had the experience of interviewing the world's top executives for national television networks.

I'm not telling you this to brag about my experience. But here's the simple truth about the media: as journalists, we need you to explain your story simply, clearly, and concisely. A dose of passion doesn't hurt. In fact, many spokespeople you see on television or read in print are not the most qualified experts on a particular topic—but they are among the best communicators of that topic. There's nothing wrong with that. A message is meaningless if nobody understands it or wants to hear it. Chrysler's Lee Iacocca, who became a model for the CEO as spokesperson, once said, "You can have brilliant ideas, but if you can't get them across, your ideas won't get you anywhere." For some reason, most executives don't quite get it. That's why you'll stand apart by identifying and absorbing the 10 Simple Secrets. Adopt them and your message will carry more power. In my experience as a journalist and corporate presentation coach, I find that those who believe they need communication training the least often need it the most.

Sorry, but You're Being Compared to Steve Jobs

Try this: Next time you watch CNBC or read the business section of your local newspaper, start paying attention to the businesspeople you see quoted. You'll notice the same names and faces keep showing up. There are so few truly outstanding spokespeople that the media return to the same speakers time and time again, whether or not they're the most qualified to discuss a particular topic. Out of more than two thousand interviews I've conducted over my television career, I can name about a dozen people who truly stood out. Here's the exciting part—you'll hear from many of them in the pages to follow!

Since most of us get our information from television news, it's logical that our perception of great speakers is shaped by whom we see on the small screen (or big screen for those of you with a fifty-two-inch plasma display). I've got news for you—great corporate spokespeople have raised the bar of what it means to be a business communicator and you're being compared to them. When CNBC interviews Apple CEO Steve Jobs or legendary General Electric CEO Jack Welch, you're being compared to them. When C-SPAN brings British Prime Minister Tony Blair into our living rooms every week, you're being compared to him. When former Hewlett Packard CEO Carly Fiorina presents a dazzling PowerPoint show, you're being compared to her. The simple fact is that most speakers who shine on television are extraordinary presenters in virtually any type of situation—keynotes, speeches, staff meetings, product launches, board meetings, or shareholder conferences. It's because they've mastered the 10 Simple Secrets. Cisco CEO John Chambers and California governor Arnold Schwarzenegger are two such examples.

★ ★ ★

"Television has set the style of a modern communicator—relaxed, informal, crisp, quick, and entertaining."
Fox News chairman Roger Ailes in *You Are the Message*

Taking the Golden State by Storm

During the course of writing this book, I had a rare opportunity to cover the first one hundred days of Arnold Schwarzenegger's administration as the new governor of California. As a reporter for Viacom-owned KCBS 2 and KCAL 9 in Los Angeles, I enjoyed extraordinary access to this magnificent speaker, his communications staff, and his best friends and advisors. As I watched Schwarzenegger persuade voters to back his vision, I reached the conclusion that he had nailed each and every one of the 10 Simple Secrets. Now, anyone who has only seen Schwarzenegger in the movie *Terminator* might argue this point. After all, he has all of seventeen lines of dialogue in the whole movie! *Saturday Night Live* loves to poke fun at him. Let's be honest, "The Governator" has a funny ring to it. But the Arnold that I saw day in and day out had extraordinary presentation skills—techniques that can turn lackluster business presenters into truly awesome speakers. Schwarzenegger certainly has passion. He's also inspirational, prepared, brief, clear, and looks like a leader.

Early in his campaign, pundits dismissed Schwarzenegger as another Hollywood actor playing politician. But by the end of his first six months in office, former critics, political opponents, media elitists, and journalists began to sound like they should work on his PR team. For an analysis seven months into the Schwarzenegger administration, a research director for the Public Policy Institute of California wrote that Schwarzenegger "wowed an adoring public." On his first anniversary of taking office, Schwarzenegger continued to enjoy astounding approval ratings. A headline in the *San Francisco Chronicle* blared "Schwarzenegger Winning Over Skeptics." Even the man he kicked out of office, former California governor Gray Davis, couldn't help but praise him saying, "Schwarzenegger has taken the town by storm." What I found remarkable about Schwarzenegger's first year is that most of his impressive list of accomplishments and public policy victories were the direct result of winning over key audiences—voters, lawmakers, and interest groups.

What's So Sexy about Internet Plumbing?

At the peak of the technology stock boom, few CEOs were more inspiring than Cisco's John Chambers. Chambers was capable of wowing audiences around the globe—from college students to analysts to heads of state. More than four million investors took notice, driving Cisco's stock to $82 a share and making it, for a short time in the spring of 2000, the most valuable company in the world.

His appearances sold out faster than a Rolling Stones concert and the audience showed no less enthusiasm for his speeches than they would for the first few notes of "Satisfaction." It was extraordinary. During one speech I attended, an audience of at least one thousand grizzled high tech veterans sat with their collective jaws dropped for twenty minutes, glued to every word. The gasps were audible as Chambers shared a vision for how the Internet would change the way we "live, work, play, and learn." Everyone in attendance stood up in a sustained round of applause as Chambers ended his talk. His presentation was second to none. It's impossible to tell how many shares of Cisco were purchased the next day from people in that room, but online broker Charles Schwab placed at least one order for one hundred shares of Cisco. Guess from whom?

One year later the bloom had fallen off the Internet rose. The NASDAQ, made up mostly of high tech stocks, had plummeted 80 percent and Cisco's stock was no exception. As Chambers himself is fond of saying, Cisco went from sixty miles an hour to zero in the blink of an eye, forcing the company to cut more than six thousand people. Cisco didn't fall off the map for a simple reason: unlike most dot-coms selling nothing but marketing fumes, Cisco's Internet hardware was critical to the growth of the Internet. It continued to generate billions in revenue. But while investors had lost interest in the stock for a time, they didn't lose interest in Chambers and his vision for how his company's products would change virtually every aspect of our lives. As a corporate pitchman, Chambers was still winning 'em over.

Despite the decline in the company's revenue and stock price, commentators continued to acknowledge Chamber's charisma, optimism, and ability to leave audiences spellbound. A *New York Times* reporter attending a Chambers speech in June, 2002, wrote, "Many people in attendance remained convinced that Cisco's best days were not behind it." *Fortune* magazine, which rated Chambers among the twenty-five most powerful business leaders, said that "listening to a John Chambers speech today is an astonishing experience."

How does Chambers create this "astonishing" experience? Was he born with the gift? Far from it. Growing up dyslexic, Chambers had to conquer his fear of public speaking. He sought extensive coaching and prepares diligently for every presentation. But the rewards are great. As of this writing, Cisco has regained momentum; growing revenue, expanding into new markets, and announcing its first major hire in three years—one thousand people. According to Cisco's vice president of corporate positioning Ron Ricci who generously gave his time for this book,

> Our employee retention is better than other companies in the industry. Our internal employee polls show they trust and believe in John Chambers. Also look at the valuation of Cisco's stock. It's a reflection of Wall Street's belief in your future. I think you can argue that Cisco's multiple is higher than it would be if you didn't have someone like John Chambers at the helm of the company.

★ ★ ★

According to Starbucks chairman Howard Schultz, the rules of engagement have changed for corporate leaders. "It's never been as important to have a base of employees who trust the leaders they work for," says Schultz. Trust is a theme that comes up time and again in my personal interviews. In the wake of corporate shenanigans like we saw at Enron, Tyco, and Worldcom, employees, customers, and investors are placing a premium on trustworthiness, authenticity, and integrity. The corporate communicators interviewed for this book rank high on the trust scale because they put people first. American Express financial advisor Tom Moser says it best: "If you throw yourself unselfishly into helping other people get what they want in life, and you are successful in doing that, you'll get every selfish thing in life that you want."

A Billion-Dollar Idea

Scott Cook, who offered his insights for this book, is considered one of the most successful entrepreneurs in corporate America today. In 1982, Cook's wife complained about the tedious task of paying bills and balancing checkbooks. Cook knew there had to be an easier way. He randomly called people in the phone book and learned that most people were like his wife—they hated it. That sparked an idea—Cook would create a software program to automate the process. Today, the company he started, Intuit, is the number one maker of bill-paying and accounting software. Its flagship products, Quicken, QuickBooks, and TurboTax, are the world's leading financial and accounting software programs. Intuit has seven thousand employees, $1.6 billion in annual revenue, and has turned Cook into a billionaire.

Prior to taking their company public in March of 1993, Cook and Intuit CFO Eric Dunn embarked on a series of road shows to convince skeptical institutional and professional investors to buy the stock. According to Cook, "Checkbook software was not the most electrifying subject for technology investors. We had to grab their attention." Cook started his presentations by asking a question: "Raise your hands if you pay bills." Of course, all hands shot up. "Now keep your hands up if you like paying bills." The response was immediate and, as you would expect, nearly every hand went down. In this way Cook reached his audience, not through words alone, but by making an emotional connection to change their way of thinking—their belief systems. "The goal of communications is to change beliefs," Cook told me. "Sometimes the most effective tool to change beliefs, deeply rooted beliefs, is to change experiences."

Cook's well-crafted, powerful, and passionate presentations paved the way for the hugely successful IPO. Investor demand was enormous. According to the *San Francisco Chronicle* on March 13, 1993, Intuit intended to sell shares at between $15 to $17 but "raised the price because demand seemed strong." The stock closed at $31 on its first day, making Cook worth $140 million on paper.

According to Cook, the company's revenue and profit growth gave investors "permission" to believe in the promise of his software, but Cook's presentations "created" the belief and convinced investors that it was for real. Cook had mastered the 10 Simple Secrets of the world's greatest business communicators and now shares his insights with all of us.

By identifying and adopting the Simple Secrets that made Cook's presentations so successful, you will be better armed to start changing the belief systems of your audience—whether it's an audience of one or one thousand. It's a powerful skill that I believe will allow you to accomplish more than you've ever imagined.

★ ★ ★

"Anybody who is living and breathing has areas they love. The key is to align what it is you really love with what it is you are communicating. If you talk to Scott Cook, Steve Ballmer, or Carly Fiorina, you'll find they love their companies and what they are doing. They love the opportunity to talk about what they do and to engage people in it." James Citrin, Global practice leader, Spencer Stuart

How to Get a 78 Percent Response Rate

Not all of the business presenters in this book run *Fortune* 500 companies, but they credit their speaking skills for much of their success. Tom Moser is a senior financial advisor at American Express. He's also a member of the President's Advisory Council—a group made up of the top 1 percent of American Express advisors. Not bad given the fact that AE has ten thousand advisors! Moser believes "the majority of success in your career will be the direct result of the quality of your presentations." Moser's presentations are so compelling that he teaches other financial advisors how to improve the quality of their talks. They listen to Moser because his presentations get results. An astounding 78 percent of the people who attend his free seminars sign up for consultations.

Whether you're a financial advisor, consultant, salesperson, manager, executive, or CEO, presentations are critical to your career success. Think about how many presentations you give every day—face-to-face with a potential client, in the elevator with the boss, at a staff meeting, in a conference, or over the phone. You're presenting constantly. How do you come across? Are you dull or dazzling? The techniques described in the pages to follow will help you craft and deliver your message with power, passion, and persuasion.

While the vast majority of CEOs, executives, leaders, and experts fail to rise to their full potential as communicators, I believe you can harness the 10 Simple Secrets in this book to stand alongside the world's greatest communicators—inspiring everyone in your personal or professional life to buy into your message.

Three Levels of Communication

Best-selling business author Geoffrey Moore, who also reveals his presentation secrets in this book, says there are three levels of communication:

1. Do no damage. This spokesperson simply wants to get through a presentation without doing harm to his reputation.
2. Get your listeners to care. This spokesperson gets the audience to actually share her excitement about the service, product, company, or cause.
3. Change the way your audience sees the world. This spokesperson connects so well that he actually changes the way his audience looks at the world. "When people say Apple CEO Steve Jobs creates a 'reality distortion field,' that's precisely what they mean," says Moore.

The *Dilbert* Principle of Presentations

DILBERT reprinted by permission of United Feature Syndicate, Inc.

The presenters profiled in this book speak at Moore's "level three." They create "reality distortion fields." It's where you should want to be. But it takes commitment. Scott Adams created the hilarious *Dilbert* comic strip that pokes fun at corporate cubicle-dwelling life. When I learned that he co-owns one of my favorite local restaurants, I contacted him to see if he would lend his humor to this book. I'm glad he agreed. I think his humor strikes a chord with readers of two thousand newspapers in sixty-five countries because it hits so close to home. Anyone working in the corporate arena has run across some or all of the characters that appear in the *Dilbert* comic strip.

"Check around," Adams says. "Fifty percent of presentations in corporate America are not intended to transmit useful information. They're intended to transmit the idea that you know what you're doing and you have things under control." That's not speaking at Geoffrey Moore's level three. Great business communicators focus on the audience, not their egos.

If your goal is simply to get to the end of your presentation, this book is not for you. It's meant for the other 50 percent—those speakers who intend to inspire, persuade, and motivate their employees, shareholders, customers, or colleagues. It's meant for contemporary communicators who want to wow twenty-first-century audiences!

If you're ready to join the ranks of the world's best corporate presenters, then let's begin the journey by identifying the first three Simple Secrets of the world's greatest business communicators.

PART ONE

GET 'EM TO CARE

You may have an incredible story to tell, but your audiences won't listen if you don't build rapport with them first. They have to like you. If they feel a connection to you, they'll listen. Contemporary audiences crave speakers who have passion, who inspire, and who exude charisma. You'll know how to get those qualities by the end of part one.

In this section you'll learn:

- How to develop a powerfully passionate presentation
- How to inspire people to achieve goals they never thought possible
- How to prepare your presentation by getting into the heads of your listeners so effectively that they can't help but follow you

Getting your audience to care requires that you identify and adopt three Simple Secrets shared by the world's greatest business communicators. Let's begin by revealing the first Simple Secret that will set the foundation for your extraordinary transformation.

SIMPLE SECRET #1: PASSION
USE YOUR HEAD TO REACH THEIR HEART

"My television shows are passionate. I get more passionate every day."

SUZE ORMAN

STARBUCKS COFFEE COMPANY

There are few things I enjoy more than a café latte—double shot, non-fat. I'll order a grande on most days, a venti when I need the extra boost. Add some caramel flavoring and there's nothing better. If you've ever stepped foot in a Starbucks, you know exactly what I'm talking about. What does this have to do with the world's greatest business communicators? Plenty. My life wouldn't be the same without a trip to Starbucks. But while I enjoy coffee, Howard Schultz is passionate about it.

"When you're around people who share a collective passion around a common purpose, there's no telling what you can do."

STARBUCKS CHAIRMAN
HOWARD SCHULTZ

Really passionate. His passion convinced investors to buy into his concept of bringing Italian-style cafés to America—and without it, I never would have been introduced to a mocha frappuccino!

During a now-famous trip to Italy, on a piazza in Milan, Schultz's life would be forever changed upon his first sip of espresso and steamed milk.

The Italians were passionate about their coffee, he excitedly told his wife. Schultz brought that passion back to America and transformed a small Seattle coffee-bean store into an American institution. As chairman and CEO of Starbucks, Schultz became a wealthy man, with an estimated net worth of over $1 billion dollars, and altered the habits of some twenty-five million people who visit a Starbucks every week.

Schultz majored in communications, took public speaking courses, and credits much of his ability to win over investors, customers, and employees to his magnificent presentation skills. "Magnificent" is my word, not his. Great communicators don't call themselves great communicators. But they touch our hearts with their passion. Some do it without ever using the word. Others, like Schultz, use it all the time.

Before I interviewed Schultz for this book, I read his best-selling business book, *Pour Your Heart into It.* I was struck by the fact that the word "passion" appears on nearly every other page. His passion is authentic because his enthusiasm and energy carry over into his presentations—to shareholders, employees, or journalists like me. All of the business leaders profiled or interviewed for this book share this quality—an authentic, unbridled passion for what they do. Contemporary audiences are hungry for it.

Schultz doesn't leave his passion on the pages of a book. "You either have a tremendous love for what you do, and passion for it, or you don't," Schultz tells me.

> So whether I'm talking to a barista, a customer, or investor, I really communicate how I feel about our company, our mission, and our values. I've said this for twenty years—it's our collective passion that provides a competitive advantage in the marketplace because we love what we do and we're inspired to do it better. We want to exceed the expectations of our people and our customers. In order to do that, you have to have a passionate commitment to everything. Everything matters, Carmine. When you're around people who share a collective passion around a common purpose, there's no telling what you can do.

The Difference Starts with Passion!

Schultz is a persuasive, inspirational business speaker—capable of convincing investors, employees and customers to believe in his vision. Schultz shares the same fierce passion for his message that all great communicators have for their respective services, products, companies, or causes. It's the most common trait shared by everyone whose secrets are revealed in this book: entrepreneurs like Schultz, Scott Cook (Intuit), Barbara Corcoran (The Corcoran Group), Jeff Taylor (Monster.com), Marc Benioff (Salesforce.com), or Richard Branson (Virgin Group); CEOs like John Chambers (Cisco Systems), Steve Jobs (Apple Computer), Jack Welch (GE), or Carly Fiorina (Hewlett Packard); political leaders like Arnold Schwarzenegger, Tony Blair, Leon Panetta, Condoleezza Rice, Nelson Mandela, or Colin Powell; or best-selling business authors like Geoffrey Moore (*Crossing the Chasm*), James Citrin (*The 5 Patterns of Extraordinary Careers*), or Suze Orman (*9 Steps to Financial Freedom*). As communicators, passion sets them apart. Whether you see them on television, listen to their speeches, watch their presentations, or talk to them over the phone, they exude passion. So should you.

Famed Silicon Valley venture capitalist John Doerr has said that he looks for a climate of passion in the start-ups he ultimately decides to invest in. Passion is the first step to building rapport with your listeners; getting 'em to care. Whether you're the CEO of a *Fortune* 500 company or an intern in the mailroom, passion will set you apart from your competition. Don't bother reading the rest of this book if you're not committed to taking ownership of this simple secret shared by all great communicators. Without passion, you're finished as a speaker. Without passion, you will fail to tell your story with confidence, charisma, and power. Without passion, you will fail to sell your message and motivate your audience to action.

The Passion Quotient

Nearly everyone can increase what I call his or her "Passion Quotient," or PQ—the level of passion you exhibit as a speaker. The higher your PQ, the more likely you are to build a strong rapport with your listeners.

By boosting your PQ, I'm not implying you turn into Italian movie director Roberto Benigni, standing on chairs and hugging members of the audience as he did on his way to accept the Best Actor Academy Award for his work in *Life Is Beautiful*. Yes, he's passionate. But he's a comedian. That's what he gets paid to do, and his audience expects it. I'm not suggesting you put on a wedding dress to promote a new venture like Richard Branson did to launch Virgin Brides or engage in an arm-wrestling match to settle a business dispute like Southwest's Herb Kelleher. They're mavericks. It's what audiences expect from them. You'd look like a fool if you tried to emulate these antics—with one exception: you're trying to build a reputation for being a rebel in a buttoned-down business. Of course, that's rare. There's plenty of room to be unique, different, and electrifying while remaining within the acceptable standards of your particular industry. But that's not to say we can't adopt some especially spellbinding techniques of some of the business world's greatest rebels.

★ ★ ★

In his book *Straight from the Gut,* Jack Welch, the legendary CEO of General Electric, says passion separates the A players from the B players. He says A players should be given raises two to three times higher than B level players.

At its core, passion simply means this: touching the hearts of your listeners by identifying a deep emotional connection to your story and sharing that enthusiasm with your listeners. This is the Simple Secret behind building a strong rapport with your audience—whether it's an audience of one or one thousand.

In the book *The Eye of the Storm*, author Robert Slater describes Cisco CEO John Chambers as "passionate and electrifying." Money managers have been quoted as saying people would walk through fire for the guy. Would people do the same for you? If the answer is no, then your message might be missing its spark, its passion. Find it.

Think about it. John Chambers didn't become a corporate star because he runs a company that sells routers, switches, and other hardware you never see. Howard Schultz didn't become one of the most admired leaders in business today because he blends the right mix of espresso, streamed milk, and foam. Emeril Lagasse didn't become a celebrity chef because he cooks a mean dish of pasta. John Madden didn't sign a $30 million contract with ABC because he coached a football team in the '70s. Oprah Winfrey didn't become the most powerful woman in entertainment because she hosts a daytime talk show. Richard Branson didn't become one of the most exciting entrepreneurs in the world because he started an airline. Suze Orman didn't become the best-selling personal finance author because she teaches people about irrevocable trusts. And Arnold Schwarzenegger didn't become the leader of the world's fifth largest economy because he has twenty-one-inch biceps. All of these people have high PQs. They communicate their messages with enthusiasm and energy—passion!

PQ Boosters	$\uparrow$ Enthusiasm + $\uparrow$ Energy = $\uparrow$ PQ

Unbridled Enthusiasm

The dictionary defines passion as "unbridled enthusiasm." Enthusiasm first found its way into the English language in 1603 and literally meant "possession by a god." Its more contemporary definition is "a strong liking for something." You probably wouldn't be doing what you're doing if you didn't like it. At least I hope you haven't settled for that path in life. I haven't met you but I'm making an assumption—you wouldn't be trying to improve your skills as a communicator unless you truly and deeply cared about your message. So I'm assuming you have a "strong liking" for the story you want to share, but are you "possessed" by it? The world's greatest business communicators are. And they show it. Enthusiasm simply means sharing your excitement about your service, product, company, or cause.

★ ★ ★

Enthusiasm: Possession by a god; Strong liking for something.

It's Not in the Beans

I can hear you saying to yourself, "That's great, Carmine. Be more enthusiastic. But how?" The simplest way to show enthusiasm is to identify and share your emotional connection to your message. Dig deep to find your own personal connection to your story. Remember, the secret to discovering your passion is to find the object of your enthusiasm. Let's be clear on this—the object of Howard Schultz's enthusiasm isn't the sweet aroma of dark-roasted coffee beans. It's the sense of community he creates in each Starbucks store, the "third place" between work and home, as he likes to call it. It's his enthusiasm about creating a company that treats employees with dignity. That's what fuels his passion. It's not in the beans.

The QVC Queen

There are approximately six hundred fifty thousand financial planners in the United States alone, yet only one holds the record for most books sold in an hour on QVC—Suze Orman. She's one of the few who can make zero coupon bonds exciting. A QVC merchandising manager once said that Orman makes viewers feel as though she's talking directly to them through the TV. That doesn't surprise me. Orman radiates enthusiasm because she has a far deeper connection to her topic than any financial expert I've interviewed in my fifteen plus years of television news. And I've interviewed a ton of people as an anchor, host, and business correspondent for CNN, Fox, CBS, CNET, and Ziff Davis Media. The nation's top financial experts know what they're talking about. But Orman stands out where most fail—getting 'em to care. They simply can't match Orman on the PQ scale.

I've interviewed Orman several times on television and specifically for this book. Her passion is contagious. That's the beauty of passion—it rubs off on your audience. Orman has a deep and personal connection to her topic that she shares with her listeners. She still carries the scars and stigma of growing up poorer than her poor neighbors and watching her father fail at one business after another. In one vivid memory, her father ran into a burning building to retrieve a cash register with less than $100 in it. It's that kind of personal experience that fuels her message—she wants everyone to reach financial freedom.

★ ★ ★

Orman doesn't turn off her passion behind the scenes. She enters a room like a whirlwind, chatting up everybody from makeup artists to camera operators. Prior to our interviews, I watched Orman as she made everybody feel like the most important person in the room at the moment and that she genuinely cared about that person's financial well-being. She's passionate, authentic, and dynamic!

Keeping the Spice Alive in Your Presentations

Today, Orman is on a mission to convince people that debt is bad; not exactly groundbreaking advice. Even Orman admits that her books don't contain revolutionary advice. "Anyone can know this material," she told me. "It's how you communicate the material you know that sets you apart."

Think about it. That's a powerful statement. It's how you communicate the material that sets you apart. No, Orman's material might not be groundbreaking, but there is something compelling about her approach to presenting the subject. She demystifies financial talk. She makes money exciting. If Orman weren't passionate about her subject, her advice would fall flat. She exudes passion every time she speaks—on television, over the phone, or in front of a large audience.

"Where does your passion come from?" I quizzed Orman.

"Passion comes from love," said the colorful financial guru.

It's like when you first meet somebody and you're attracted to him or her. Passion rises up in you. You make love every day, you come home and everything is passionate about that person. Six months go by, then two years, and the passion is gone. And now you're lucky if you make love every three months! It's like a chore. Why does the passion leave? Where does the passion come from? It comes from a newness, Carmine. Newness gives you passion. Every time I talk about something, it's like the first time I've ever talked about it. So, it's new to me even though I've said it one and a half million times already. It sounds new to me and since it feels new to me, it feels like a new affair to me. So, I'm excited to tell you about it because it sounds like the first time I've ever said it! My TV shows are passionate and emotional. My passion picks up as hours go by. I get more passionate every day.

As you can probably tell, Orman has an engaging personality. But it's interesting to watch financial planners fall over themselves to duplicate her personality and style. They try, and most fail. They simply don't share her passion—her emotional connection to her topic.

According to Orman, "If you want to strike a universal chord and get somebody's blood pumping, you've got to appeal to the heart before you appeal to the brain. Otherwise, you will put them to sleep. You will have an intellectual conversation and before you know it, their eyes will start to close. You will have bored them to death. If you involve their emotions, you now have passion!"

Listen to the words Orman uses time and time again: "I'm on a mission…I'm on a crusade." What's your mission? What's your connection to your story? Dig deep, find it, and express it!

★ ★ ★

I was writing this book during the 2004 presidential primary season. Nine candidates were running for the Democratic nomination. Massachusetts senator John Kerry would eventually win the nomination but lose the general election. Early on in the campaign, while all the talk focused on the then-front-runner, former Vermont governor

Howard Dean, one man caught my attention because of his captivating speaking style—North Carolina senator John Edwards. I knew very little of the man but, as I had said to myself about Arnold Schwarzenegger when many people were writing him off, Edwards had an amazing ability to connect with people. The BBC called Edwards an "accomplished orator." His skill served him well—Edwards finished second and was tapped by Senator John Kerry to be his vice-presidential running mate.

When I first watched Edwards, I found him to be very passionate. I wasn't quite sure where it came from until I read his story. He had been a successful trial lawyer when his sixteen-year-old son, Wade, was killed in a car accident. A devastated Edwards gave up his lucrative law practice to run for the Senate—something Wade had urged him to do. Edwards said Wade's memory fueled him, giving him a passion for politics. It showed.

In an interview for the March 8, 2004, edition of *People* magazine, former White House press secretary Joe Lockhart said, "He [Edwards] has a Clinton-like ability to connect with people…they like him—that counts for a lot." In *Time* magazine Edwards said, "The only way you can effectively communicate is if people feel that you're real."

Who Said a Virgin Can't Have Fun?

Few business professionals are more enthusiastic than British entrepreneur Sir Richard Branson. On second thought, no business professional exudes more passion than Branson. If you can name one, please let me know! Branson commands the $7 billion Virgin empire which he started from scratch as a teenager. Today the Virgin Group contains some of the most recognizable brands in the world including Virgin Atlantic, Virgin Megastore, Virgin Mobile, Virgin Cola, and some 224 other companies. How he juggles all of these ventures is a mystery to me. What's clear is how he's mastered the 10 Simple Secrets beginning with passion!

Branson is a favorite media subject; whether it's for CNBC or *Fortune* magazine, journalists seek him out for one reason—he has fun. Few entrepreneurs are more engaging. In an interview for *Fortune* magazine, one executive said "all Richard has to do is sneeze and he's all over the front page." How does he get there? He has fun, he's passionate, and customers love every minute of it.

Like another successful CEO, John Chambers, Branson is dyslexic. He readily admits that when he is asked to talk about a subject he knows little about, he gets uncomfortable. But as he writes in *Losing My Virginity,* when asked to speak on something he feels passionate about he's "reasonably fluent." I'd say that's an underestimation, which is out of character for Branson!

An article in London's *The Independent* once quoted a psychologist who said one-third of the people he surveyed did not have passion in their lives. "Passion has long been associated with brilliance and success," said the expert, pointing to examples like Branson and his passion for building companies. I think he's partly right. Passion and success are closely related. But he loses me when he says one-third of people don't have passion. Give me a break. We're all passionate about something. Great communicators are better at recognizing what they're passionate about and transferring that passion to their listeners. On the surface, Branson may seem passionate about starting companies from scratch and turning them into global brands. But dig deeper. He's passionate about having fun while he's doing it. Branson started Virgin Atlantic because he was tired of high fares and poor service at existing airlines. He wanted to put the fun back into air travel. "Fun," Branson writes, is one of his "prime business criteria." Branson has a deeply held belief that "every minute of every day should be lived as wholeheartedly as possible."

Just as Schultz uses the word "passion" in his conversations, Branson uses the word "fun." Regardless of the words they use, both entrepreneurs are enthusiastic about what they do and their enthusiasm is contagious. Branson is an exceptional communicator because he transmits his passion through his actions as well as his words. Whether it's dressing up in a wedding gown for the launch of Virgin Brides or dropping into the center of New York's Times Square wearing nothing but a strategically placed cellphone for the launch of Virgin Mobile, Branson exudes a zest for life and his products. That's why we in the media love the guy. The media is so fond of Branson that Fox gave him his own reality show in 2005. *The Rebel Billionaire* was *The Apprentice* on steroids.

Branson's ability to persuade others to back his vision has been behind much of his success, from creating a student-run magazine in 1968 to starting Virgin Atlantic when the experts said he was crazy for trying to compete against British Airways. Those "experts" failed to understand a key component behind his persuasion: Branson's energy, enthusiasm, and passion are contagious. Investors want to back him, customers want to buy from him, and smart people want to work for him. That's a powerful combination of supporters! You don't have to pull a stunt for your next prospect meeting. I'm fairly certain you won't land customers by rappelling down the side of their building (another Branson caper). But take at least one lesson from the Branson playbook—show 'em you're having fun. They'll notice.

He's Back!

California governor Arnold Schwarzenegger has mastered the 10 Simple Secrets of the world's greatest business communicators. Most observers, on the left or right of the political spectrum, are beginning to recognize Schwarzenegger's talents as a passionate, persuasive, and powerful presenter. Like Branson, Orman, Chambers, and Schultz, Schwarzenegger's impact as a speaker is rooted in a deep passion for his mission. Whether it's to become the world's best bodybuilder, the biggest box-office star, or the governor of California, Schwarzenegger's ability to stir his audiences begins with PASSION. I can name dozens of athletes, movie stars, and politicians who don't come close to matching his level of enthusiasm. It's captivating and it's a big part of his magnetism.

Schwarzenegger builds a stronger rapport with his audience than just about any presenter I've seen or interviewed. I covered Schwarzenegger's first one hundred days for CBS in Los Angeles. I watched him dazzle virtually everyone—from voters to political opponents to the world-wide press who converged on Sacramento to cover his first days in office. They melted in his presence. Schwarzenegger won 'em over by being direct, enthusiastic, and passionate.

No one would argue that Schwarzenegger doesn't have passion—the fire in the belly that separates all great communicators. But where does it come from? What made him give up the multimillion-dollar paychecks to run the state of California? (He earned $30 million for *Terminator 3,* making him the highest paid actor in history.)

The Schwarzenegger secret is simple: he has a deep, personal, and emotional connection to his message and never hesitates to share it with his listeners. Schwarzenegger's poor upbringing in a small Austrian hamlet fuels his intense ambition and fierce determination. In an interview for *Parade* magazine he said, "Being from poor circumstances gives you a lot of drive. My mother sometimes had to beg for food. We had no phone, no indoor plumbing, no car. It was rough." His upbringing explains his will to succeed, but his passion comes from his desire to give something back to the country that allowed him to live his dreams.

In February of 2004, I watched Schwarzenegger as he spoke to a group of two thousand high school students at the Sacramento Convention Center. They asked him why he had given up his movie career to run the state. His explanation reflects the passion behind his message, his emotional connection to the topic. "I wouldn't have any of it if I hadn't come to California," Schwarzenegger said.

> America and California gave me everything. Now is the time for me to give something back. From the time I was a boy, I had a clear vision that I would become a world champion bodybuilder and be in movies. I went way beyond my dreams. As I moved up in my career, and I won all those championships and made all that money, I was thinking of myself: "How can I be the most muscular man? How can I get into movies? How can I be the richest guy?" Then I said, "I have to give something back."

And give back he did. In 1989, he got involved with the Special Olympics and became the chairman of the President's Council on Physical Fitness and Sports. He said he experienced more joy working with disadvantaged youth than making movies. "For the first time, I looked beyond myself," Schwarzenegger said. "I wanted to give something back to my country and the millions of people who need help."

Ten years ago, Schwarzenegger founded the Inner City Games Foundation to offer America's youth some exciting activities they could do after school, when many are the most susceptible to joining gangs, taking drugs, or getting into trouble. In *Parade* he said,

When I came over to America, I was absolutely convinced that if I can make it here, anyone can. Then I traveled to all fifty states, visited inner-city schools, saw hopelessness, ghetto kids, beaten down latchkey kids drifting, saw kids without the childhood that will create the drive and confidence that I had. It was clear to me that kids who do not have that foundation cannot be successful. They needed help. This was the turning point for me.

Every communicator has a turning point that fuels his or her passion. The world's greatest business communicators take it one step further—they express it. It's this Simple Secret that helps them build a rapport with their listeners. For Schwarzenegger, it was his work with inner-city kids and with the Special Olympics. For Orman, it was watching her father sink further and further into debt. For Schultz, it was a visit to a magical place, Milan, Italy.

What was your turning point? What gave you the passion to do what you're doing? Dig deep, find it, and express it!

★ ★ ★

Media mogul Oprah (do you really need her last name?) once said, "Your true passion should feel like breathing. It's that natural." Oprah has become a media sensation because she shares a deep connection with her viewers. They feel as though she's their best friend. They all know her painful childhood secrets and struggles. In every show, every interview, every magazine article, she reinforces her personal connection to the particular topic. When launching her enormously successful book club, she said, "Books were my pass to personal freedom. I learned to read at age three, and soon discovered there was a whole world to conquer that went beyond our farm in Mississippi."

Energy Boost Please!

Energy is a close cousin of enthusiasm. You can't talk about one without the other. It would be like discussing the success of Elton John without Bernie Taupin, or Dean without Jerry or *American Idol* without Simon Cowell. You just can't do it. Energy conveys enthusiasm.

As Billy Joel once sang, "She's got a way about her." That's what energy is—a way about you, a way of building rapport with your audience and getting 'em to care. Are you alert, animated, vigorous, and expressive? Great business communicators, whether they're soft-spoken or boisterous, exude energy—vigor, vitality, and an intensity of expression.

Ronald Reagan had energy. Cisco's John Chambers has it, as does Oracle CEO Larry Ellison. Former General Electric CEO Jack Welch has it, as does Southwest's Herb Kelleher. Virgin's Richard Branson has it, as does Microsoft's Steve Ballmer and Apple's Steve Jobs. They all have very different speaking styles, but they all have energy and enthusiasm generated by a deep connection to their message and a burning desire to share their passion with the rest of the world.

Savvy leaders exude youthful energy. We've all heard about the efforts John F. Kennedy took to hide his substantial ailments from the public. In comparison, Kennedy's predecessor, Dwight Eisenhower, was low-key and less robust. Ike built his reputation as a war hero but Kennedy was the better presenter. Every leader since Kennedy has had to learn the lesson— energy wins people over.

I recall my first interview with Vice President Al Gore, when he was still a senator from Tennessee. I couldn't help but notice he wore some light makeup, well aware of the bright camera lights and how they can wash out a speaker. While my photographer was setting up his camera, Gore seemed listless and tired. I choose to believe it had less to do with my personality than it had with a late vote the night before. Regardless, when the time came to shine, he did. He was "on." Gore threw his shoulders back, stood up straight, held his head high, put a warm smile on his face, and turned up his energy level a few notches. He transformed right before my eyes.

Gore gets it. So does Schwarzenegger, although I think he's always energetic. In the halls of the state capitol, Schwarzenegger smiles warmly, walks briskly, and vigorously shakes hands with friends, colleagues, supporters, and visitors. One of his senior advisors once told me that Schwarzenegger has more energy than anyone who works for him. That's the point—energy and enthusiasm reflect your passion and it rubs off on your listeners. We gravitate toward communicators and leaders who have energy.

You can have all the passion in the world, but if you don't have the energy to express it, then nobody will share your enthusiasm. There are three simple ways to increase your energy: It's all in the way you sleep, eat, and think.

★ ★ ★

Energy Boosters:
• Get Plenty of Sleep
• Eat Well and Keep Fit
• Maintain a Relentlessly Positive Attitude

Get Your Zs

According to the National Sleep Foundation, two-thirds of us do not get the recommended eight hours of sleep and one-third get less than six hours. "Chronic lack of sleep drains natural energy reserves, causing slow thinking, impaired memory, erratic behavior, mistakes, and irritability," writes Pamela Smith in *The Energy Edge*. While it's true that some great communicators get by on less than five hours of sleep (Oprah, Bill Clinton, NFL head coach Jon Gruden), most great presenters perform best after a good night's rest. Don't fight it, just do it—especially prior to important presentations.

When it comes to getting enough snooze time, it pays to know yourself. Ronald Reagan did. On his last day in office, former president Jimmy Carter was said to have phoned Reagan on the morning of Reagan's inauguration to bring him the latest news on the fifty-two American hostages being held in Iran. Keeping meticulous notes, Carter noted that at 7:00 a.m., he placed a call to Reagan who, in keeping with tradition, was staying at the Blair House across the street from the White House. According to *Reagan on Leadership* author James Strock, an aide told Carter that Reagan had "had a long night, was sleeping, and was not to be disturbed. 'You're kidding,' an incredulous Carter replied. 'No sir, I'm not,'" came the reply.

There are two ways of looking at this story. A Reagan critic might easily say, "you see, Reagan was intellectually lazy." But the purpose of this book is to not to make political judgments—it's to identify and help you adopt the Simple Secrets shared by the world's greatest communicators.

According to Strock, "Reagan trusted his staff's judgment to protect him from an interruption of sleep that would have served no purpose in achieving the release of the hostages…but could have made him less rested as he approached one of the most important speeches of his life." The fact is that newspaper articles about Carter's last day described him as looking tired, haggard, weary, and in bad health while Reagan looked like, well, a movie star—rested, energetic, vibrant, robust, and healthy—despite being the oldest president at seventy years of age. Reagan knew himself. He had mastered the Simple Secrets that would turn him into "The Great Communicator."

Fuel Your Mind, Work Your Body

A poor diet and lack of exercise will kill your energy, leaving you tired, listless, and less powerful as a presenter. Scott Norton is a personal trainer and CEO of Axis Performance Center in Menlo Park, California. His clients include some of the top corporate leaders in Silicon Valley, many of whom are fantastic spokespeople. "Getting on a proper training program will help you have better posture, exude more energy, and prepare you to handle the demands of a busy professional life," says Norton.

"Without energy, you'll look and sound like a dud. But if one executive trains regularly, he'll look and feel energized. He's passionate. He's at his best. He radiates health and vitality. The one who doesn't train, who doesn't watch what he eats, might be a competent executive but doesn't radiate the same kind of energy."

In Simple Secret #9, we'll talk much more about health and fitness as it relates to great communicators—you'll even learn about the Ultimate Presentation Diet! For now, keep in mind that diet and exercise will affect your health, weight, mood, and energy level. Eating well and keeping fit are critical to becoming a high-impact communicator. The right foods will keep you healthy and energetic. Exercise sends oxygen-rich blood cells to the brain, which results in clear thinking. Clear thinkers are better speakers.

Relentlessly Positive Thinking

In 1953, Norman Vincent Peale launched the classic *The Power of Positive Thinking*. Peale was one of the first authors to make the connection between your health and the way you think. He also demonstrated how the power of positive thoughts could boost your energy. In his book, Peale recounted the story of a politician who still had boundless energy after seven speeches in one day. When asked why he wasn't tired, the politician said, "Because I believe in everything I said in those speeches. I am enthusiastic about my convictions." According to Peale, "That's the secret. He was on fire for something. He was pouring himself out and you never lose energy and vitality in doing so. You only lose energy when life becomes dull in your mind."

Military hero and former secretary of state Colin Powell lives his life with unshakable optimism. Powell has said that "perpetual optimism is a force multiplier." Powell's presentations reflect his perpetual optimism. Oren Harari, author of *The Leadership Secrets of Colin Powell,* interprets Powell's quote to mean "a leader's enthusiasm, hopefulness, and confidence multiply as they radiate outward…leaders who view the world positively and confidently tend to infuse their people with the same attitude." Harari credits Powell's optimism for his ability to rally his troops and the American public. "There is clear evidence that people resonate with leaders who offer positive messages," says Harari.

★ ★ ★

"Unlocking human potential is what leadership is all about. When human potential starts to manifest, it comes with increased passion, energy, and enthusiasm."
George Zimmer, CEO, Men's Wearhouse

In politics, research shows that optimistic candidates have the advantage. In his studies at the University of Texas, Austin, Professor Bruce Buchanan has found that pessimists have a difficult time winning. If people resonate with optimistic speakers, then it's no coincidence that Governor Schwarzenegger won over California voters. He's the poster child for positive thinking. When I sat down with Schwarzenegger's communications director, Rob Stutzman, for a lengthy interview about the governor's first one hundred days Stutzman said, "Schwarzenegger is an incredible optimist. He wants to inspire people to achieve, whether he's speaking publicly or meeting with us privately. The wrong answer is always—'it can't be done.' He will not accept it. It defines who he is. This is how you come to dominate your sport, your industry, or politics."

Paul Wachter, Schwarzenegger's long-time friend and business advisor, works closely with the governor on a variety of matters. "His speeches are always optimistic," Wachter told me. "They reflect who he is. They reflect his enthusiasm, optimism, and vision. It's not a coincidence that he uses the word 'fantastic' every twenty seconds. We kid him about it. But it's his strength. He is unwilling to look at the down side of things."

Here's the bottom line on energy—great business communicators have it in abundance. Each and every one of them. I don't care what you do to boost your energy—get more rest, exercise, eat better, or watch Dr. Phil to improve your attitude. The fact is that too little sleep, a poor diet, and a bad attitude are energy killers. As a person trying to unlock the secrets of great communicators, you can't afford to be anything but your best.

By now I hope you're convinced that passion is the fundamental building block of all great communication, business or otherwise. Electrifying business speakers are passionate about what they do and they show it. Dale Carnegie may have said it best in *How to Develop Self-Confidence and Influence People by Public Speaking:* "If your desire is pale and shabby, your achievements will also take on that hue and consistency. But, if you go after your subject with persistence and with the energy of a bulldog after a cat, nothing underneath the Milky Way will defeat you!"

After Reagan's passing, syndicated columnist David Broder wrote, "Because he could persuade almost anyone of anything, changes that would otherwise have been impossible to imagine did happen. And the world is profoundly different because of him." Imagine the changes you could make in your company, industry, or personal life if you could persuade almost anyone of anything! People liked Reagan because he had confidence, vision, and optimism, unfailing optimism—he believed in the American dream and, more importantly, made people feel as though they could achieve it themselves.

Now that I've challenged you to raise your PQ, it's time to reveal the Second Simple Secret of the greatest business communicators.

★ COACHING DRILLS ★

1. **Watch How Others Do It.** Visit www.carminegallo.com for profiles and video clips of passionate corporate communicators. Then ask yourself:

• How can I tell they're passionate about the topic?

_____

_____

_____

_____

_____

• What is their connection to the topic?

_____

_____

_____

_____

_____

Compare their energy level to yours. Rate them on a scale from 1 to 10, with 1 being as dry as Melba toast and 10 being over the top. Where do they fall? Where do you stand? Videotape your presentation or listen to your voice on a phone voice recorder. Rate yourself on the energy scale. Most of my clients start out at 2 or 3. Can you bump it up to a 6, 7, or 8? I bet you can. Your presentation will be stronger for it.

_____

_____

_____

_____

_____

2. **Connect to Your Topic.** Becoming a passionate speaker will be easier if you understand your personal and emotional connection to your topic. By answering the following questions, you'll be using your head to reach the hearts of your listeners.

- Why do you believe in your service, product, company, or cause? Why should your listeners care?

_____

_____

_____

_____

_____

- What's your connection to your story? Think about your cultural background, childhood or adulthood experiences, encounters with colleagues, anecdotes, etc.

_____

_____

_____

_____

_____

- Have you shared this connection with your audience? If not, how can you incorporate it into your message?

_____

_____

_____

_____

_____

SIMPLE SECRET #2: INSPIRATION
C'MON BABY, LIGHT MY FIRE

"I can inspire people to do things I believe in."

MICHAEL JORDAN

Fitness Publications, Inc.

"If you show people what's coming and how to get there, it changes everything. You have to have wisdom."

CALIFORNIA GOVERNOR
ARNOLD SCHWARZENEGGER

On the night of August 6, 2003, during a taping of the *Tonight Show with Jay Leno,* a bombshell hit California politics. Action-movie star Arnold Schwarzenegger announced he would challenge current governor Gray Davis in a recall election set for October 7. Having seen Arnold speak to large groups of business professionals, I knew August 6 would go down as the worst night in Davis's political career. Where Davis had all the charisma of a squid, Arnold radiated it. Sixty-two days later, millions of voters swept a sitting governor out of office for only the second time in American history. An unprecedented 135 candidates vied to replace Davis. Arnold got 48 percent of the vote. His closest opponent, Lt. Governor Cruz Bustamante, came in a distant second with 31 percent of the ballots cast.

Immediately after Schwarzenegger's victory speech, an NBC correspondent covering the event in Los Angeles said, "His charisma. His ability to work a crowd. That's a big reason for why he's here tonight." Two years earlier, I sat in an audience of corporate types as Schwarzenegger captivated a crowd of twelve thousand people at the legendary Bakersfield Business Conference. It didn't take me long to realize "The Terminator" had mastered every one of the 10 Simple Secrets of great communicators—he grabbed 'em, hooked 'em, and blew 'em away. Arnold's oversized success in bodybuilding, movies, business, and politics had little to do with twenty-one-inch biceps and everything to do with drive, confidence, and charisma. He inspired people to believe in him and his vision. He won 'em over!

Schwarzenegger exudes unshakable self-confidence, infectious optimism, self-deprecating humor, and a passion for the initiatives he embraces. Schwarzenegger's confidence convinced him to throw his hat in the ring and his optimism helped him maintain his resolve against a daily barrage of criticism, but it was Schwarzenegger's charisma that inspired voters and won the election.

Never underestimate a great communicator's ability to inspire audiences. Outside of California, and for many people inside the state, the very thought of Governor Schwarzenegger seemed like a joke. Not anymore. Only six months into his role the staid British magazine *The Economist* praised Schwarzenegger's accomplishments, saying "what a short, strange, surprisingly pleasurable trip it's been…the idea of Governor Schwarzenegger no longer seems so weird." A *New York Times* editorial on Tuesday, May 4, 2004, acknowledged that "this page was among the vocal doubters…nobody's laughing now."

Captivating Charisma

I've never seen the term "charisma" more closely associated with a leader than in the first six months of the Schwarzenegger administration—with one exception: Ronald Reagan.

"Schwarzenegger's public charisma, private charm and upbeat, nothing-is-impossible demeanor are very Reaganesque," wrote Dan Walters in the *Sacramento Bee*. "And, like Reagan, Schwarzenegger was underestimated," he adds.

Charisma is the key to inspiration. By definition, charisma is a "personal attractiveness that enables you to influence others; an ability to arouse fervent popular devotion and enthusiasm." That's inspiration. Inspiring leaders and business executives have the rare ability to touch their listeners, motivate their audiences, and elicit that "fervent popular devotion."

Arnold's charisma factor intrigued me. If everyday business presenters could capture this magic in a bottle, I thought, imagine how effective they would be in winning over their audiences. Just imagine.

I decided to break down the specific traits that separated Schwarzenegger from most public communicators. Sometimes events really do unfold for a reason. Just as I undertook this research, CBS hired me to cover the Schwarzenegger administration for its affiliates in Los Angeles. This access gave me a unique perspective into Schwarzenegger's character and his communication secrets.

The Seven Habits of Highly Charismatic Leaders

Stephen Covey may have introduced us to the seven habits of highly effective people, but I chose to identify the secrets behind the world's most highly "charismatic" corporate speakers. The first thing I did was to conduct an analysis of media coverage with the help of my associates at Gallo Communications Group. During the sixty-two-day campaign, a staggering total of 17,509 articles were written about the recall election. "Charismatic" was the most common adjective used to describe Schwarzenegger, showing up in more than three hundred articles in just two months. Most of those articles compared Schwarzenegger's charisma to Davis's lack of it. Let's take a closer look at the specific words used to describe Arnold and Gray Davis.

Where Arnold was seen as warm, passionate, and electrifying, Davis was viewed as cold, unemotional, and colorless. It probably didn't help that Davis's first name was Gray, but with a name like that, he should have worked harder to add color to his presentations. Even more detrimental to Davis's image: Arnold was described by supporters and opponents alike as having a "commanding presence" while Davis was labeled as "stiff" and "wooden." Davis's entire persona could be summed up by his words and actions during his concession speech. Davis kept his emotions in check, which I think reflects his failure to build rapport. *San Jose Mercury* reporter Scott Herhold wrote, "There were no tears, no recrimination, no evident bitterness…and maybe that's one reason people rejected him. The guy didn't seem human."

Leader 1: Arnold	Leader 2: Gray
• Warm	• Cold/Distant
• Animated	• Monotone
• Passionate	• Unemotional
• Energetic	• Listless
• Easygoing	• Reserved
• Electrifying	• Colorless
• Commanding Presence	• Stiff/Wooden

If you want to join the ranks of the world's greatest contemporary business communicators, then seem human. Twenty-first-century audiences want to see what you see. They want to feel what you feel. If you can get them to care about your message, you can get them to take any action you want. That's inspiration. Humans, by nature, want to improve their lives, the lives of their children, the lives of others. It makes no difference if you're facing the boss or the board, senior managers or employees, existing clients or potential customers—your audience is made up of human beings who want to be inspired. Charisma alone doesn't win over audiences, but it gets 'em to care about the speaker and the message—it builds rapport.

★ ★ ★

"Charisma...is now regarded as essential for career success," according to the *Times* of London (January 30, 2003). "Jack Welch at GE, Steve Jobs at Apple Computer, and Virgin's Sir Richard Branson are all examples of charismatic business leaders. They radiate a personal magnetism that attracts employees and customers alike."

Paint a Picture

The words journalists use to describe Schwarzenegger reflect his charisma. Charisma opens doors. Charisma inspires. But let's be more specific. What is at the heart of inspiration? What exactly is the Simple Secret to motivating everyone in your personal and professional life? The secret behind this powerful ability is striking in its simplicity: inspiring business speakers are artists. They paint a picture of a world made better by their service, product, company, or cause.

JetBlue CEO David Neeleman turned an upstart discount into a major carrier with $1 billion in revenue in just four years. Passengers all get leather seats and access to satellite TV. Unlike their experience on many other airlines, JetBlue passengers are greeted by courteous, knowledgeable, and attentive staff. Yes, charging low fares helps, but if it weren't for JetBlue's impeccable service it would be another struggling discount airline instead of winning awards for offering the best quality of an U.S. airline. It starts at the top with a CEO who treats his employees with dignity and who inspires them to higher levels of achievement. Neeleman has said, "Tell your employees, 'let me paint you a picture of what we're trying to accomplish,' and then people will walk through walls for you." Would people walk through walls for you? Paint them a picture first. Stick to it, and they just might.

Think about it. Cisco's John Chambers doesn't pitch Internet routers and switches, the hardware his company manufacturers. He promotes a world in which the Internet changes "the way we live, work, play, and learn." The fact that his company's hardware makes it possible provides the subtext to his presentations, but first and foremost he sells a dream— a dream of a better life. Howard Schultz makes his money off coffee beans—whole, ground, or otherwise—but what he's really selling is a blend of coffee and romance. Schultz has succeeded in painting a picture of comfort and community—a "third place" we can enjoy between work and home. In the same way that Chambers and Schultz pitched their respective companies to investors, Schwarzenegger pitched his vision to his audiences—painting a picture of a better California for voters, their families, and future generations.

Like all great communicators, Schwarzenegger is a master at promoting his vision. Like all great communicators in politics or business, he wins over his audiences by painting a picture so bright that people can't help but follow. "I came to America with nothing and California gave me everything," he would say. His message was simple and his vision was clear: California had lost its luster. By working together, we could return the state to the "golden dream by the sea" with plenty of jobs, lower taxes, and a healthy business environment.

During an interview with Marshall Loeb for *Fortune* magazine, former GE CEO Jack Welch was asked what qualities he looks for in men and women he promotes in the company. Welch answered, "You clearly want somebody who can articulate a vision. They have to have enormous energy and the incredible ability to energize others. If you can't energize others, you can't be a leader." Welch has also been quoted as saying, "Good business leaders create a vision, articulate the vision, passionately own the vision, and relentlessly drive it to completion." Create the vision and articulate the vision passionately—that's the secret to inspiring and motivating your listeners.

It's no coincidence that Schwarzenegger and Reagan are often compared. Reagan knew the key to inspiring people was to get them to buy into his vision. Reagan painted a vivid, simple, and inspiring picture of where he wanted to take his audience—taxes had to be cut, government had to shrink, and communism had to be defeated. Regardless of whether you agreed with his vision or not, it was simple, direct, understandable, passionate, and consistent. It's what he believed and it struck a chord with a majority of Americans at the time. In *Reagan on Leadership,* James Strock writes, "If the vision is understandable, credible, shared, and compelling, the people will join the leader and move forward together.... Reagan always understood the single most important role of a leader is to craft a compelling vision."

In an interview with *Esquire* magazine in July 2003, Schwarzenegger said, "When people walk away with a vision, it changes the whole picture, it shows them what we can accomplish. That's what Kennedy did; he provided a vision. If you show people what's coming and how to get there, it changes everything. You have to have a vision." Every success in Arnold's life started with a vision. At fifteen, he had a "vision" of himself as Mr. Universe. He achieved that dream five years later. Same thing with coming to America, becoming a movie star, and owning businesses—it all started with a vision. It's why he looked remarkably unconcerned about negative stories during the campaign. In his own mind, he had already won the election.

Shortly after the Schwarzenegger election, I interviewed Martin Gagen, the executive director of 3i, one of the world's largest venture-capital firms. According to Gagen, "Arnold's big belief is that 'politics as usual' has ruined the state. So I'm going to make this a 'people state' again. When you listen to him, for a moment, you think it's just political rhetoric. But when he starts talking about how he arrived to this country as an immigrant and his desire to give something back to his adopted country—his beliefs come through. He telegraphs his core beliefs."

Gagen says the best presenters in his business—those who have the best chance of getting venture capitalists interested in their ideas—paint a picture of how their products, ideas, or companies will make the world a better place. "If you believe you're going to transform the world, you need to tell people the mission you're on. I really like listening to someone who has a view of the world slightly different than everyone else. If they have a strongly held belief, a passion, they can convince you to look at the world as they do."

During the 2003 California gubernatorial recall election, businessman Peter Ueberroth dropped out early when polls showed him far behind. Although his resumé was filled with accomplishments like building successful businesses, serving as National League baseball commissioner, and spearheading the 1984 Olympics in Los Angeles, he simply failed to connect with people whom he asked to vote for him. His persona didn't match his operational skills. Many reports pointed to his "lack-luster" presentations as a reason for his failed attempt to lead the state. Sometimes an awesome resumé isn't enough.

Mandela Had a Road Map

Few visions have had as profound an impact as Nelson Mandela's "dream of an Africa which is in peace with itself." Mandela spent more than twenty-seven years in prison for fighting to improve the plight of black South Africa during a time of white minority rule. Mandela was set free after South Africa abolished apartheid. He was awarded the Nobel Peace Prize and served as the first black South African president after winning the country's first multi-racial election.

The years he spent in a notorious Cape Town prison only strengthened his resolve to change the way his countrymen lived together. His vision saw him through those years and inspired hundreds of millions of people in South Africa and around the world. Your vision might not be as grand as a world in which race and color don't matter, but it proves that a big and bold vision cannot be underestimated. Mandela had a road map: he knew where he wanted to lead his people and how to get there. What's your road map? Where do you want to take your company? How will you get there? Above all, have you communicated this vision to the people who serve with you? Mandela painted a compelling vision. He's an artist who transformed the hopes and aspirations of the people who followed him. By painting a compelling vision of a bright future, you too can lead others in your mission.

The Broken Ankle That Inspired a Corporate Empire

The world's greatest business communicators paint pictures by telling inspiring stories. You'll find that each of the great business communicators interviewed for this book uses stories to paint a vivid picture of their vision.

The very first line of Howard Schultz's book has nothing to do with Starbucks, but in a sense has everything to do with it. The first sentence of *Pour Your Heart into It* reads, "On a cold January day in 1961, my father broke his ankle at work." The story of how his father's injury left his family with no income, no insurance, and no safety net to cushion the blow marked a turning point in Schultz's life.

Schultz consistently tells this story to employees, journalists, and shareholders as a way of inspiring his audiences to back his vision. I wanted to know more about that story when I spoke to Schultz.

"What does your dad being laid up by a bad ankle have to do with roasting coffee beans?" I asked.

"On many levels, the experiences I had as a young child formed my values and my understanding of what it meant for people to be left behind," Schultz responded.

Starbucks employs eighty thousand people. We hire three hundred people a day and open three new stores a day. It's very important new people understand that when I started this company I had nothing—what drove me then and what drives me today is to build a different type of company, to create an environment in which people are respected and dignified in the workplace. Starbucks is the quintessential people-based business. I've always thought it was important that people have a sense of my own vulnerability as well as what it is we're trying to achieve as a business.

I asked, "Do you think by sharing these stories you inspire your employees, shareholders, and partners?"

"I think so." He responded.

It goes against the past tradition of business leaders. But it's important that people understand who you are, why you act a certain way, and respond to things in a certain way. Be a man of the people. If you look at some of the great leaders in history, they had the gift of galvanizing large groups because people saw in them something that resonated. To do that, you have to let people in—take off the shield.

After the scandals we've seen at companies like Enron, Tyco, and Worldcom, it's more important than ever for contemporary communicators to let people in, to "take off the shield."

One of the top CEO recruiters in the world, Spencer Stuart's James Citrin, agrees that Schultz inspires by sharing stories.

"The story about his father—it provides the underpinning for stock options and full health benefits for all employees, even part-timers," says Citrin.

> When he tells the story about how he went on vacation to Italy, got entranced by the espresso-bar culture, and believed that he could transport that kind of community—that was the seed of the Starbucks strategy. He brings the stories to life. To get the most out of people they're working with, leaders have to tap into their emotions as well as their minds. People can relate to stories. They can see themselves in other people's stories. I would bet that when Howard Schultz introduced the Bean Stock program [stock options to turn employees into partners] in a board meeting, he told the story about his father. The ability to use stories to get people to buy in with their hearts is a powerful leadership capability.

When I interviewed Howard Schultz, I asked him how he won over investors who funded the original concept for Starbucks. "The presentation was everything," he said. "But it was the substance and the unbelievable commitment we demonstrated early on about our feeling about the business. We never viewed this as work or a business. This was our life. We love this company. We are passionately committed to what we're doing, the way we're doing it, and we wanted to change the world." Schultz says he never would have accomplished his goals for Starbucks if it hadn't been for his "partners," the employees—but it was essential that they share a common vision.

Walking All the Way to the Bank

There's some dispute as to whether Akio Morita invented the Walkman on his own. But there's no disputing that he turned the device into a mega-sensation and propelled the company he cofounded into the number one consumer electronics brand in the world—Sony. As a technology visionary, Morita has permanently earned his rightful place as one of the giants of industry.

Morita's passion and vision are legendary. After all, here's the guy who said, "Our plan is to lead the public with new products rather than ask them what kinds of products they want. The public does not know what is possible, but we do." How's that for vision? He's absolutely right, of course. Morita saw millions of consumers hooked up to portable music players, playing video games on their TVs, and chatting on cell phones well before the rest of us did. He saw Sony selling gadgets ranging from $20 radios to $20,000 plasma televisions.

Morita was so convinced that his small radio manufacturing company could become a global brand that he once declined an early offer from Bulova for one hundred thousand radios because they would carry the Bulova name. It was an "incredible order," worth several times the capital of the entire company. In turning down the order, Morita promised that in fifty years, the Sony brand would be just as famous as Bulova was at the time. When Morita's company created a miniature transistor radio in 1958, only one percent of Japanese homes had a TV set, yet Morita was introducing personal consumer electronics to this population. That takes vision. Sony, however, would still be a tiny blip on the corporate radar if it hadn't been for Morita's ability to sell his vision.

Morita inspired his audiences to go along for the ride even when they were skeptical about his ideas. In his autobiography, *Made in Japan,* Morita talks about his efforts to convince his colleagues that consumers would buy a portable media player that would let them listen to music via their headphones—the Walkman. "It seemed as though nobody liked the idea," wrote Morita.

The Sony CEO had one great advantage: he knew how to tell a good story. Morita told the story of two shoe salesmen in the jungle. One reported back to his superior that none of the natives wore shoes and that there was no market there. He took the next flight home. The other salesman recognized the potential and told his boss, "None of the natives wear shoes; we can clean up the market here. Please send all available stock and as many salesmen as you can muster!" That's classic Morita. He recognized an untapped market and communicated his vision through stories meant to inspire his colleagues, customers, and shareholders.

Morita was adamant about inspiring his employees. "In the long run," he writes, "no matter how good or successful you are or how clever or crafty, your business and its future are in the hands of the people you hire. To put it a bit more dramatically, the fate of your business is actually in the hands of the youngest recruit on the staff." Morita believes a manager's results are best measured by how well he or she can organize a large group of people and focus that group on getting results. Morita writes, "If the workers lose their enthusiasm for the company the company may not survive." Morita told stories to convince his colleagues, shareholders, and employees of the potential for new products. All the great business communicators in this book share this trait: they articulate their message in a way that it can be understood, remembered, and acted upon with gusto. They tell stories. Stories make people feel good about the company and the spokesperson.

Great business communicators tell inspiring stories, and we all have inspiring stories to tell. My training as a journalist has taught me to find the story in any situation. A newscast has to make air. Since when has the five o'clock news been canceled because no news happened that day? If it's a "slow news day," I'm still responsible for a story. A good journalist can always find one. So can you. There's a story behind your service, product, company, or cause. It's there. You just have to look for it. The communicators in this book tell inspiring stories that are personal, vivid, and reflect a big mission.

Take It Personally

We've just gotten started, but think about how many stories we've heard from the world's greatest business communicators that have something to do with their childhoods: Howard Schultz and his father's struggle in corporate America, Suze Orman and her dad's money trouble, Schwarzenegger and his journey to California. They all tell personal stories.

I had the pleasure of interviewing former White House chief of staff Leon Panetta, who served under the Clinton administration. Panetta has enjoyed successful careers as a lawyer, congressman, chief of staff, and now as head of the Panetta Institute in Monterey, California. He has a charming and outgoing personality. He's a fabulous communicator who tells personal stories constantly. When I asked him how he approaches public policy, he said he pursues policies that are in the best interest of our children. "I'm inspired by my father," he said. "As an Italian immigrant, when he came to this country, everything he did was to carve out a better life for his children. I believe it's how public policy makers should make decisions—by answering this question: what makes the most sense for future generations?"

I've always liked Panetta since the first day I met him as a young television anchor in Monterey, California. I can relate to him through the stories he tells—he built an instant rapport with me. He's proud of the foundation his immigrant parents provided for him. As am I. My parents came to America with nothing, moved to the Bronx, and later to California. My dad, who was a prisoner of war from the ages of sixteen to twenty-one, believed in providing his kids with the finest education. He sent me to UCLA and Northwestern and my brother to the Georgetown School of Medicine. Francesco Gallo may not have had a lot of money when he first came to the United States, but he had a big vision!

Personal stories don't always have to do with growing up; far from it. But they should have something to do with a personal experience. Devin Wenig is a president and executive director at Reuters, a 150-year-old media company in the process of reinventing itself in an industry dominated by twenty-four-hour cable news and the Internet.

"You can either minimize or maximize the substance of your story with the way in which you present it," said Wenig. "I often move into personal anecdotes about why things are working, and why other things are not working." For example, Reuters is reducing its product line from thirteen hundred products to thirty-five. That's a deep change, which could easily cause disappointment, frustration, and confusion among employees and customers. Wenig is an inspiring leader and communicates the transition through personal stories.

I tell the story of about a year ago when I walked into a client's office, a customer. He had the Reuters price list which he rolled out across the conference room table. He said, "Would you please interpret this for me because I have no idea what I'm supposed to buy and frankly, your salesperson has no idea what he is supposed to sell." Of course, I had no clear answer on that. It was clear to me exactly at that moment that there was an opportunity cost. This mass confusion was strangling the company. It's a simple story that communicates the point about why we're making a change to our strategy.

★ ★ ★

When asked what he'd remember about Ronald Reagan, the former secretary of state George Schultz said, "He was a great believer in the way to make his point clear is to tell a story. He wanted people to imagine themselves in the story and they'd get his point."

A Snarling Pack of Dobermans

In 2001, Cornell University conducted one of the most exhaustive studies of leadership, charisma, and inspiration. For leaders, they chose U.S. presidents. What they found was extraordinary, but of no surprise to anyone who understands why the great business communicators profiled in this book radiate magnetism. The Cornell study concludes, "The successful articulation and enactment of a leader's vision may rest on his or her ability to paint followers a verbal picture of what can be accomplished with their help." Sound familiar?

According to the Cornell study, the most effective way of painting a verbal picture involves the use of image-based rhetoric. "Leaders who use words that evoke pictures, sounds, smells, tastes, and other sensations tap more directly into followers' life experiences than do leaders who use words that appeal solely to followers' intellects." In other words, charismatic spokespeople use words that evoke sensory experiences to connect on an emotional level—words like "dream," "sweat," and "heart." Recall Arnold's "dream" of a new California? Martin Luther King Junior's "dream" of a color-blind society?

Great contemporary business communicators are masters of using vivid imagery. A recent media campaign for Cisco's 3700 router compared the hardware to a snarling pack of Dobermans with the power to protect your network from the inside, outside, and everywhere in between. It can "sniff out" who is on the guest list and deny entry to those who aren't. That's imagery! And it's certainly more exciting than describing a piece of hardware for routing Internet traffic in highly technical language. In fact, the more complex your service, product, company, or cause, the stronger the need for vivid language. During a Comdex speech, Hewlett Packard's Carly Fiorina used image-based rhetoric to reinforce the fact that HP's products touch all of our lives: "We're in a lot of places you see every day," she said. "If you made a city of all our customers, it would be twenty-one hundred times larger than Las Vegas." Now that's a compelling image.

Image-based words will help you win over your audience for several reasons:

- You'll grab and keep their attention. Images are concrete. Abstract concepts are harder to follow and tougher to remember. They fail to inspire.
- You'll stick with your audience long after your talk. People can't act on something they don't remember. Vivid images inspire. They are richer experiences that will stick in the minds of your listeners.
- You'll reach their heart. Most people will not act on messages that fail to connect with them on an emotional level. According to Cornell researchers, "Leaders who infuse their messages with image-based words will, therefore, evoke a stronger emotional response among followers, increasing followers' willingness to embrace their visions and, ultimately, to act."

In *The New Imperialists,* Mark Leibovich explains why Cisco CEO John Chambers originally took a sales job at IBM when his background was better suited for marketing or operations: "The company wasn't selling products as much as it was selling dreams—dreams of a business process made more efficient. It was a philosophy that allowed Chambers to peddle hope and possibility, which was far more

The Big Mission: First Why, Not How

Leave it to *Dilbert* creator Scott Adams to knock management's vision—or the lack of it. Adams told me that most managers fail to articulate a clear and compelling vision because they don't have anything to say! Well, this chapter assumes you have something to say. But Adams has a point—you first need a road map. Having a vision is half the battle. The battle will be lost if others don't follow you. People crave direction and they're more than willing to take the road less traveled as long as they know why they're taking the road.

Great business communicators share the why before the how. Apple founder and CEO Steve Jobs is a master of inspiration. He radiates a charisma that captivates thousands of the "Mac faithful" as well as customers, employees, and colleagues. Jobs co-founded Apple in 1976 and ignited the personal computer revolution by launching the Apple II and the Macintosh. After a long exile from the company he formed, Jobs made a dramatic return to Apple in 1997 and nurtured it back to health. Jobs is currently Apple's CEO as well as CEO of Pixar, the award-winning animation studio that made *Toy Story, A Bug's Life, Monster's, Inc.,* and *Finding Nemo.*

★ ★ ★

Jobs continues to reinvent the Apple brand. Boosted by sales of 4.6 million iPod digital music players in 2004, Apple's stock hit an all-time high of $80 a share in January of 2005 and the company is on track to make $13 billion by the end of the year.

Jobs has a reputation as being one of the most charismatic, captivating pitchmen in corporate history. According to Alan Deutschman in *The Second Coming of Steve Jobs,* "he was the master of taking something that might be considered boring—a hunk of electronic hardware—and enveloping it in a story that made it compellingly dramatic." Whether at Apple or Pixar, people wanted to work for Jobs because they found his big mission intoxicating.

"Our noble purpose is bringing people together to advance their lives. Our mission is to be the world's leading career center that works with job seekers, employers, employees, and shareholders who want to participate in our story."
Jeff Taylor, founder, Monster

Sell Sugared Water or Change the World

Jobs incorporates many subtle techniques into his presentations (techniques that will be revealed in coming chapters), but the key to his success as a communicator is his nearly messianic zeal to change the world. That's the road he's on. In the case of Apple, he passionately believed that he was not creating a new computer box, but an experience. In the case of Pixar, he convinced his team of engineers, executives, and designers that they were on a mission to reinvent movie animation. By painting such a compelling vision of the future, it's no wonder that Jobs can persuade bright people to work for him, investors to believe in him, and customers to buy from him. He's out to change the world, and isn't too bashful to admit it.

A famous story about Jobs dates back to March 1983. The brash twenty-eight-year-old entrepreneur was sitting on a terrace overlooking the Hudson River with forty-four-year-old John Sculley, then president of Pepsi. In an effort to recruit Sculley to Apple, Jobs turned to him and said, "Do you want to spend the rest of your life selling sugared water, or do you want a chance to change the world?" That's brash. That's bold. That's optimistic. That's a big mission.

Describing a big mission simply, concisely, and passionately is important to telling inspiring stories. Jobs didn't have trouble raising capital in his life because he knew how to share his big mission. It's critical, says venture capitalist Martin Gagen:

> We get many technology companies who spend an hour talking about their technology and product when all you want to ask them is—what is the defining purpose of your company? I don't want to know what you make but what does it do, what does it change, why is it relevant to anybody in the world? What is your mission in

life? If it's exciting, then you can tell me more about how your company will get me there.

Gagen's observation is right on and it's shared by the majority of venture capitalists I've interviewed as a journalist—the best presenters inspire their audiences by following this simple rule: First why, not how.

★ ★ ★

"The best leaders have employees who follow them anywhere…they understand results are achieved not because they have the perfect strategy or know how to give orders, but because the people who work for them feel empowered to do their very best."
Carol Hymowitz, *The Wall Street Journal*

If you think about it, you'll find that all great business communicators have a big mission they use to inspire, motivate, and persuade their audiences. Let me drive this point home by sharing more stories of great leaders who articulate a big mission.

Dell Direct: From Dorm Room to Your Door Step

Michael Dell dropped out of college and started his computer powerhouse with $1,000 from his own pocket. At the age of eighteen, he clearly saw an opportunity, understood how to exploit it, and successfully communicated the vision to others. Dell became the youngest CEO of a *Fortune* 500 company. In his book, *Direct From Dell,* Michael Dell succinctly outlined his vision:

> Here was a device [the personal computer] that so profoundly changed the way people worked—and its cost was coming down. I knew that if you took this tool, previously in the hands of a select few, and made it available to every big business, small business, individual, and student, it could become the most important device of this century…I knew what I wanted to do: build better computers than IBM, offer great value and service to the customer by selling direct, and become number one in the industry.

How's that for a big mission?

Get Big...Fast!

For its twenty-fifth anniversary issue, *Inc.* magazine featured their list of the top twenty-five entrepreneurs. Among the list were Intuit's Scott Cook and Amazon's Jeff Bezos. Bezos was chosen for his vision. He was thinking so big when he started his online bookstore even the name he chose, Amazon, conjured up something huge! The story is well known by now—how Bezos hammered out his business plan in the car during a cross-country trip with his wife. Even though he wanted to start as an online "book service," Bezos knew it would grow out of just selling books. He wanted a name that didn't place limits on his ambition or the company's potential. Bezos started the company with $300,000 from friends and his own bank account. But he used big, bold, and optimistic rhetoric to convince twenty local Seattle investors to pitch in $1 million, before the "Internet boom" boomed. Tom Alberg, an early Amazon investor, recounted the story in *The New Imperialists*. According to Alberg, "He [Bezos] came off as this likable guy with an unshakable belief in what he was doing." For a corporate mantra, Bezos chose a phrase that best reflected his big mission—Get Big Fast.

Martin Gagen praises Bezos for the emotional connection he makes with audiences. "When you think of the best speakers, think of Amazon. You can have all sorts of issues with his business, but Bezos is laughing, smiling, evangelical. No matter what you think of his business model, you can't help but like the guy and say to yourself, he's engaged. His presentation style is 100 percent emotional. You want to listen to the guy." Do people want to listen to you? They will if you tell them why! You've got plenty of time for the how after you've grabbed 'em.

Give 'Em More Than a Paycheck

During our interview at the Intuit campus, CEO Scott Cook said,

> It's important to communicate a bold vision for many reasons. Primarily for internal reasons, for the people in your company. Your people want to know that their work is adding up to a great cause. They want more than a paycheck. They want to know that

they are making a big difference in the world. And they will believe a bold vision. It's very important to getting the best people—that you have a bold vision and communicate it well. Unlike a bus, you can't drive a company alone. Everyone has to drive one part of the company, and they all have to drive the parts to the same destination. The most important audience is the people in your company.

★ ★ ★

"Find ways to reach down and touch everyone in the unit. Make individuals feel important and part of something larger than themselves."
Colin Powell, *My American Journey*

Lose Yourself in Something Bigger Than You Are

When it comes to inspiration, legendary Penn State football coach Joe Paterno is second to none—the most wins for any football coach in Division 1A history, two national titles, and over fifty years at the same institution. While he's a brilliant tactician, Paterno would not be nearly as successful if it had not been for his ability to motivate his players to leave everything they have on the field.

Budd Thalman spent fifteen years as the go-between for Paterno and the media at Penn State. He wrote a book filled with Paternoisms called *Quotable Joe*. Thalman told me that well before the team even has its first practice, Paterno inspires his players by getting everybody on the same page, fighting for the same goal. "Paterno tells his players not to win for him or the university but for themselves, their families, and their teammates," says Thalman. "If everybody plays to their ability, then the whole team wins."

Listen to Paterno's own words in *Paterno by the Book*: "In teaching excellence in football, we have to reach the soul of the player. Football is played, above all, with the heart and mind…therefore, at the heart of our curriculum, as important as skills and tactics, are the purposeful uses of emotion, commitment, discipline, loyalty, and pride."

Loyalty and Pride. If you're one of Paterno's players, that's what you're playing for—the loyalty of your teammates and the pride of adding your name to the pantheon of legends who have gone before you. Well before you first see a playbook, Paterno tells you WHY you have to give it your all. Well before their first practice, Paterno will remind his players of what they're playing for: "I want you to understand that you are a Penn State football player. Ten years from now, you'll walk into an office and put your card down, and somebody will say, 'Oh, you're the guy who played at Penn State.' The players who have gone through here have respect. I want you to understand the exultation of victory…I want you to be able to look at each other in the locker room and say, 'Hey, we're national champions.' And to lose yourself in something that's bigger than you are."

The End of Software?

As CEO of Salesforce.com, Marc Benioff is a colorful, charismatic, and inspirational visionary in the corporate software industry. Salesforce competes in the $7 billion customer-relationship software industry. I had the pleasure of coaching Salesforce.com executives prior to the company's highly successful IPO.

As Internet companies were imploding around him, Benioff founded a web-enabled software company that put competitors on notice. Actually, they couldn't help but notice when sales topped $100 million just three years after Benioff launched the company. Traditional companies in the category sell packages of software that clients customize and install on their computers. Salesforce is 100 percent online, leasing the software to subscribers who pay a monthly fee. Benioff understands the value of putting himself in front of the brand, giving presentations and interviews at every opportunity. His big mission is innovative and bold, and he repeats it consistently. He calls his master plan "The End of Software." In an interview for *Selling Power* Benioff said, "A great salesperson is one who can create a transcendent vision for your customer. Draw a road map for your customer by saying, 'If you do this and buy these products, it will take you there. I want you to go there. Do you want to go with me? This is a great idea—let's do it together.' This is incredibly important today." Benioff should know. He was Oracle's top salesperson and at the age of twenty-five, became the youngest vice president in the company's history. He's done okay for himself. The Salesforce IPO went on to become one of the hottest IPOs of 2004, surging 56 percent on its first day of trading and making Benioff worth nearly half a billion dollars!

It's Good to Be Larry Ellison

Speaking of Oracle, CEO Larry Ellison, one of the world's wealthiest men, gave Benioff $1 million to help start his company. It's good to have friends like Larry. A lot has been written about Ellison, both positive and negative, but very little about Ellison's dazzling presentation style. Oracle CEO Larry Ellison built a $10 billion software powerhouse based largely on his ability to communicate his vision and inspire customers, employees, and investors. Stuart Read spent six years working at Oracle. In his book, *The Oracle Edge,* Read says that much of Oracle's success is due to Ellison's style. "Larry is fantastic at creating excitement—over and over again. He makes inspiring product announcements by talking about things people dream about. It's not easy to do if you're selling industrial database software."

Interesting, isn't it? Like Chambers, Ellison spends less time on the technology itself than on how it's going to improve your company's bottom line. First why, not how. Ellison's position as a captivating communicator is unassailable. In *Momentum,* author Ron Ricci writes, "Ellison understood how to draw attention to himself and his company by moving beyond simple product announcements…he personalized the concepts in ways virtually anyone could understand. In this way, he intuitively grasped, before many of his contemporaries did, that customers would ultimately reward him for taking risks—even when his big ideas failed."

I think these stories reinforce the big theme of this chapter. Contemporary audiences love big ideas. They crave a mission. They will follow you to the end of the race if you've fueled them with a purpose. You've got to have a purpose and, more importantly, you have to express it. What's yours? How will your service, product, company, or cause change the world, or at the very least improve the lives of your listeners? Answering this question will take you to the very heart of inspiration and to a new level as a business communicator.

★ ★ ★

On May 25, 2004, Cisco Systems introduced the most powerful router for directing Internet traffic, the CRS-1. To launch the product, Chambers gave a brilliant presentation to a group of analysts, customers, and media. As I watched the presentation, I couldn't help but think that an average presenter would have focused on the router's technical specifications: The CRS-1 router scales up to 92 terabits per second, powering the first OC-768/STM-256 IP interface and supporting up to 1152 40-Gbps line-card slots. That would have been far too technical for Chambers, who wowed his audience by offering an inspiring description of what the new product would do for them.

Chambers got their attention by saying it would change every aspect of their lives. Then he broke it down. For consumers it meant a faster Internet—giving them the power to transfer the collection of the entire Library of Congress in 4.6 seconds. For Cisco customers, like telephone companies, it meant they could connect three billion telephone calls in the blink of an eye and more calls could get through for Mother's Day or *American Idol* voting! And for shareholders, it meant that Cisco had taken the biggest jump in product innovation since the router was invented—and it was "only the beginning." That's Chambers at his best. Leave the specs for the website. Leave the audience in awe.

An Offer Suze Orman Couldn't Refuse

As we close this chapter, remember one cardinal rule about inspiration—it's not enough to articulate a big mission, you have to believe in your own mission. During a conversation for this book, Suze Orman recounted a story of something that happened to her a few years earlier. Legendary actor Marlon Brando had seen Orman's PBS special. Orman said,

> When he first saw me, he thought two things: Either this woman is the greatest actress God ever created or she is seriously the real thing because she believes what she is saying to her core. Well, he watched me for two years and decided I must be speaking the truth. He instructed his secretary to track me down to go over

some financial issues with him. A true master of acting knows when somebody is acting or truly inspired. But I'm only inspiring because I'm inspired myself. I am excited about my material. If I'm not excited, how can I expect to excite you?

Does your vision inspire you? If not, it's time to reevaluate the big mission behind your service, product, company, or cause. After all, if you're not out to change the world, there are plenty who are.

Now that you've learned the second Simple Secret of the greatest business communicators, it's time to reveal the third Simple Secret.

★ COACHING DRILLS ★

1. **Who Do You Consider Inspiring?** How does that person "paint a picture"? How does that person paint a picture of a better world?

_____

_____

_____

_____

_____

2. **Tell Your Own Stories.** What stories can you incorporate in your next presentation? Make them personal and vivid. How do they connect to the mission of your service, product, company, or cause?

_____

_____

_____

_____

_____

3. **What's Your Big Mission?** Remember, your big vision is not to sell me ten thousand units of your widget. It's to sell me on a dream—how will your widgets make me money? How will they make me more productive or help me retain employees? Show me the vision and take me there.

_____

_____

_____

_____

_____

SIMPLE SECRET #3: PREPARATION

TOSS THE SCRIPT

"No one, no matter how gifted, can perform without preparation."

RUDOLPH GIULIANI

Photo for Cisco Systems by Cour Mast,
Mast Photography, Inc., San Francisco

"He doesn't want you to feel as though you're one of five hundred people in the audience. He wants to feel like you're having a one-on-one conversation with him."

CISCO SYSTEMS VICE PRESIDENT RON RICCI
DESCRIBING CISCO CEO JOHN CHAMBERS.

Once a year in the small farm town of Bakersfield, California, about ten thousand people gather to watch the world's most influential speakers at the Bakersfield Business Conference. Everybody who's anybody in the world of business, politics, and entertainment has spoken at the event including Ronald Reagan, Jimmy Carter, Gerald Ford, Mikhail Gorbachev, Margaret Thatcher, Colin Powell, Bill Cosby, Tom Hanks, Jay Leno, Tom Brokaw, and yes, Arnold Schwarzenegger.

The most powerful speakers at the conference—the speakers who have the most success winning over the audience of business professionals—are those who are best prepared. The 2002 conference wrapped up with an inspiring speech by former New York mayor Rudolph Giuliani. One year after the terrorist attacks of

September 11, Giuliani had become a national hero and best-selling author with his book, *Leadership*. Giuliani's book and his subsequent public appearances drew my attention to the fact that the world's greatest business communicators prepare for every presentation—whether it's a speech, an interview, a meeting, or a sales call. Giuliani attributes much of his success to his relentless preparation, devoting an entire chapter of his book to the topic. According to Giuliani, "preparation is the single most important key to success, no matter what the field."

Only Maya Angelou Can Get Away with It

If I hadn't read Giuliani's book, how would I know that he diligently prepares for every presentation? The same way I can spot the best prepared presenters—they don't read from notes, scripts, or slides. During one of the now-famous board meetings at the end of *The Apprentice* on NBC, a young man-named Troy was arguing his case in front of Donald Trump, pleading with the billionaire to avoid being "fired." I remember Trump barking at Troy for relying on notes he had written on a pad. Trump said he hates it when people read from notes. Troy was indeed fired. Trump is like most listeners. They hate to watch speakers read. Contemporary audiences are won over by presenters who speak from the heart. Scripts put a wedge between the presenter and the listener.

Great business communicators toss the script to catch the audience. There is one exception to this rule—Maya Angelou. She's allowed to read her poetry. The rest of you have to lose the script if you want to capture the hearts and minds of your listeners. I've never seen Oracle CEO Larry Ellison read from notes. Ever. I've never seen Cisco CEO John Chambers read from notes. Ever. I've never seen former Hewlett Packard CEO Carly Fiorina read from notes. Ever. Neither does Giuliani.

For his first budget presentation as mayor on Feb 2, 1994, Giuliani prepared relentlessly on work-rules concessions, productivity gains, budget cuts, and revenue projections. Complicated stuff. He began the preparation in October for a speech in February! Why? So he could present it from the heart, without notes. "I gave the whole presentation without a script," writes Giuliani in *Leadership*. "Beginning with that first speech, I've always done budgets without prepared text. A few years later as my confidence grew, I began giving my State of the City address the same way." Giuliani says as a leader you might be brilliant, but you will fail to win over your listeners without careful preparation.

George Martin, the organizer of the Bakersfield Business Conference, invited me to meet with him as I worked on this book. I asked Martin which speakers made the strongest connection with the conference's audience. Martin answered, "Those speakers who prepare for their talk. No great speaker fails to have a plan. They know what they're going to say, how they're going to say it, and how they're going to end it." I think Martin is right on target. The best spokespeople know what they're going to say, how they're going to say it, and how they're going to start and finish their presentations. It's critical to building rapport—getting 'em to care.

The Best-Prepared Corporate Pitchman

If you've never seen Cisco's John Chambers give a presentation, you can watch him in action by visiting the links on this book's website. I would urge you to do so as Chambers reflects each of the 10 Simple Secrets. He is undeniably one of the most dazzling communicators in business today. *USA Today* columnist Kevin Maney believes Chambers's extraordinary communication skill is behind his ability to drive policy changes through Cisco so quickly. Maney told me, "Chambers is one of the most proactive communicators in the industry. He talks often and he talks well, using a style that's a mix of TV preacher and Oprah. He develops a message and stays on message as well as any presidential candidate. The result is that the company knows exactly where he stands and where he's leading them."

It's been said that in a room of five thousand employees, each and every person feels as though Chambers is speaking directly to them. Chambers works hard to make a connection with his listeners—building rapport with customers, shareholders, or employees. After long conversations with Cisco's top executives, I'm convinced Chambers's preparation is second to none, making him one of the most brilliant corporate orators of our time.

Ron Ricci is Cisco's vice president of corporate positioning. Ricci has worked closely with Chambers for nearly a decade, helping him craft and deliver the company's message. Ricci tells me that Chambers has evolved as a presenter by breaking the barrier between himself and his audience. He does so by preparing his material so well he internalizes what he intends to say. Doing so allows Chambers to move off the stage and literally touch the audience, physically and emotionally. Chambers moves away from the podium and into the audience, looking at them in the eye, asking questions, touching shoulders, and making everyone in the room feel as though they are having a one-on-one conversation with the man. Like a Baptist minister, the audience is his flock and he gets them to focus on the opportunity in front of them.

"Chambers is very well prepared," says Ricci. "He looks at six slides on a single sheet of paper, memorizing the bullet points and the flow of the story. He knows where his inflection points are. He knows when to pause, when to look someone in the eye, when to put his hand on someone's shoulder as if to say 'what I'm telling you right now is really important.'"

Like Giuliani, Chambers never reads from his prepared notes during a presentation, and only occasionally glances at his PowerPoint slides as he moves from one to another. Chambers, Giuliani, and the other great communicators command their material. They've mastered it, and they own it. Mastering your material requires just two actions: knowing your audience and rehearsing your presentation.

Tossing the script allows you to make that all-important eye contact with your listeners. In *The Power of Persuasion,* Dr. Robert Levine writes about the techniques used by skillful persuaders. According to Levine, "the style of presentation can be critical. People who speak confidently…are perceived as more credible. Nonverbal cues are also important. Studies show trial witnesses who stare their questioner straight in the eye instead of looking away are not only perceived to be more authoritative, but also more honest."

Size 'Em Up for Big Results

If you want to achieve unbelievable things in your personal or professional life, you need to have a bold vision (your big mission) and an unshakable belief in your ability to reach your goal. Even with a grand vision, great business communicators take it one step further. They get their audiences to buy into their vision by first learning what the audiences want, need, and expect. They do their homework first. Not one of the speakers I interviewed for this book starts a presentation without knowing more about their audience than most people know about their neighbors. They ask themselves a series of questions that allows them to build a strong rapport with their listeners before they've said their first words. Let's hear from three great presenters who size up their listeners for big results: a marketing guru, a best-selling leadership author, and a business television star.

Cross the Chasm

High-tech marketing guru Geoffrey Moore is among that rare breed of author who reaches superstar status in the business community. His book, *Crossing the Chasm,* has been called one of the most influential business books of the twentieth century. One of his books, *Living on the Fault Line,* reached the sixth spot on Amazon.com less than twenty-four hours after its release. That's serious influence. I was thrilled that Moore agreed to share his insights for this book.

Moore is a venture capital partner with Mohr, Davidow in Palo Alto, California. Since his books are required reading at the nation's leading business schools, Moore is a frequent speaker known for his engaging presentations.

During one of our conversations, I asked Moore, "What makes you so dynamic as a speaker?"

"I work from my audience back to the message," said the former English professor turned high-tech marketing guru.

"Before I speak, I grill the person who's giving the event about who is in the audience. What's on their mind? What's keeping them up at night? Then I sit down and the first two or three slides are intended to build a bridge from where the audience might be and where I need them to be in order to start talking."

Moore says he never gives a "canned" talk. Instead, he says,

I spend an hour on the phone with event sponsors to understand the context, their intent, the audience, their interests, and then brainstorm intersections between ideas and models in our practice and issues and concerns in their community. Based on that, I come up with a key theme. The net result is that with a modest amount of extra work the talk has more impact. The key is a willingness to embrace the audience's point of view as your starting point instead of simply rolling out your standard stump speech.

From Me to We

It wouldn't do justice to John Maxwell to call him a leadership author. He's a real business guru in every sense of the word: his books become instant best-sellers and he's paid big money—really big money—to speak to groups of business professionals. Maxwell has written over thirty books on leadership including *The 21 Irrefutable Laws of Leadership.* For an article on Maxwell in *The Toastmaster* magazine, I interviewed Maxwell at length about his "secrets" for dazzling his audiences. "All great communicators have one thing in common," he said. "The ability to connect with an audience. I begin all my speeches by learning as much as I can about my listeners—their hopes, fears, challenges, ambitions, and expectations." Maxwell says being able to shift the focus of a presentation from "me to we" is the essential trait shared by captivating communicators. "Instead of saying to yourself, 'here is my subject,' shift focus to the audience. Ask yourself, 'What do they want to learn from me?'"

Get into Their Heads

Stuart Varney knows the language of business. Having spent twenty-five years as a business news anchor for CNN, the *Wall Street Journal,* and now for the Fox News channel, he has interviewed the world's most influential political and business leaders including Bill Gates, Margaret Thatcher, and hundreds of others. He also makes more money for one speech than the average American makes in a year. Business leaders want to hear what he has to say. But before he begins a speech or presentation, Varney gets into their heads.

First of all, I want to know the audience: Who am I speaking to? Are they all American? Is it half European? What age are they? What's their background? What industry do they belong to? What company are they with? I want to know as much as I can about the nature of that audience. That's number one.

Then I ask myself, "How can I make them laugh?" What kind of humor would turn them on? To me, humor in a presentation is very, very important. Humor livens it up. Humor makes people feel good. So I ask myself, "What anecdotes can I introduce that are germane to that audience and will make them laugh?" That's how I start.

Once Varney understands the makeup of his audience, what makes them laugh, and what issues they expect him to discuss, the rest is easy. And it helps Varney build a relationship with his listeners. He gets 'em to care by caring about their needs, wants, and expectations.

By now it should be clear that all great business communicators spend a lot of time preparing for their presentations by getting to know their audience. Notice something—Moore, Maxwell, and Varney may approach their preparation slightly differently, but they all ask themselves a variation of those four words—why should they care? Once they answer that question, the rest of their presentations fall into place.

A study released in *Business Week* found that 96 percent of executives had some anxiety about public speaking. Remarkably, being prepared can help cut down on the presentation anxiety most of us feel. Most people are uneasy to some extent about speaking in front of groups, even small ones. Certainly an important presentation to your boss or board of directors is more likely to make your palms sweat than a talk to peers in the lunchroom. But the more prepared you are to face the press or your boss, the less nervous you'll feel. Knowing your audience, knowing your material, and taking the focus off yourself will help calm your nerves.

Three Questions to Get inside Their Heads

The world's greatest business communicators get to know their audience before they say a single word. So should you. But as we've seen with Moore, Maxwell, and Varney, they ask themselves a series of questions to get into the heads of their listeners. Let me make it even easier for you by listing three questions you should ask yourself before any type of public presentation—whether it's a meeting with your boss, a client pitch, a product launch, or a media interview. Remember, you're always presenting. Answering these three simple questions about your audience will help you soar to the next level as a corporate speaker:

- What do they need to know?
- Why should they care?
- What action do I want them to take?

The answers to these questions will help you master the material. In fact, if you only take one thing away from this chapter, make it these four words: Why Should They Care? Those four words are on the minds of every person in your audience—a boss, a board, a sales prospect, it doesn't matter. Have you ever watched a presentation at a conference where you've been positively bored to tears but considered it rude to leave since you were sitting in the front row? Painful, isn't it? If the presenter had simply asked himself those four words, why should they care, you may have survived the presentation or, better yet, actually enjoyed it! If the presenter had asked himself the other two questions, you might have enjoyed it and given the speaker your business. Now that's a winning presentation!

Adding Value to a Value Added Presentation

I recently worked with the sales team for a Value Added Reseller (VAR) that assembles computer systems based on a client's particular needs. The VAR industry is highly competitive—presentations to prospective customers are their lifeblood. This particular VAR had been in business a long time and had a great track record of success. But there were so many elements to their message, we were struggling to highlight key features and benefits that would resonate with their customers. Once we answered the three questions, however, the rest of the presentation fell into place. Here's how the coaching session went:

Q: Carmine (Coach): So guys, what does your audience, in this case a prospective customer, need to know about your service?

A: That we can save them money by reducing their IT [information technology] costs. A LOT of money!

Q: That's unique—NOT! Every VAR says that. You and the other ten thousand out there. Why should these prospects care about your message?

A: They should care because as opposed to most of our competitors, we've been in business for thirty years and we're profitable in a down market. They can rest assured that we will not go out of business. We're also experts in something called virtualization technology, which is a way to reduce server costs. If they haven't heard about it, they will want to learn more about it. And have we mentioned that our customer service is second to none? We have testimonials that will back it up.

Q: Okay, now I care. What action do you want your audience to take?

A: Set up a second meeting with our technical specialists. We know that after a second meeting, there is a strong likelihood that we will get their business.

After we spent a few minutes answering these questions, the kick-off to their presentation fell into place. Here's how it went:

Good morning. Thanks for giving us the opportunity to tell you more about our company. Who are we? We're IT cost reduction specialists. We're the nation's most advanced integrators of virtualization technologies, which I can explain in a moment. Bottom line, we can save you a ton of money. We've been in business thirty years and we're profitable. Every one of our employees is empowered to do what's in the best interest of our clients and that makes it extremely easy to do business with us. We'd be happy to have you meet the members of our team who will oversee your account. We also have an impressive list of *Fortune* 500 clients who will provide references for us. Let me tell you a story about how we helped one client avoid a potential disaster...

It's that simple. By asking three questions about your audience, you can easily establish a rapport with your listeners—getting 'em to care about your message. Remember, your goal is to get your audience to nod in agreement and to genuinely want to hear more. It's to be heard!

Barbara Corcoran turned a $1,000 loan into a New York City real estate empire. Her book, *Use What You've Got,* became a *New York Times* business best seller. During my interview with Corcoran, I asked her what she considers the one communications technique which sets her apart in her industry. She answered, "I always use stories. That's what people remember. They remember stories. Also, put yourself in the shoes of your audience. They're asking themselves, 'So what?' The only information they find of value is information they can personally use. Ask yourself what is the practical information of your point. How can they use this information? Help the audience answer the question 'So what?'"

Rehearse, Rehearse, Rehearse

Once you know your audience, rehearsing is the second and final action to mastering your material. Glancing at notes two minutes before your presentation won't cut it. Rehearsing means walking through your talk or presentation exactly as you would when you deliver it. There's a story about former vice president Al Gore who prepared for a debate with Jack Kemp by asking that the temperature in the practice room match the temperature in the debate hall the next day. Now, you don't have to take rehearsal to that extreme, but it reinforces the fact that great communicators leave nothing to chance.

Cisco's John Chambers certainly doesn't. According to Cisco vice president Ron Ricci, Chambers's preparation is relentless. The night before a presentation, he will review the slides and text. He'll take a five-mile run in the morning and practice his presentation in his mind. Before a presentation, he walks up on stage before the door opens, reviews the set-up of the chairs, and asks to see the lighting. Chambers will leave the stage to see the lighting from the audience perspective. He knows where the lights are in every section of the hall so he is never outside of the lights! He wants the audience to see him. He wants to know how he looks when he's walking down aisle A or B. He clicks through every slide to see how the flow builds. He may eliminate slides at that point. Ricci says by preparing this way, Chambers can "focus on things that separate a presenter from getting a four out of five versus a five out of five."

Failing to Rehearse Could Cost You Your Job

Failing to rehearse could lead to disaster—losing an account, losing an opportunity, or losing your job. I remember working with the vice president of a private company in Silicon Valley who had to give a major presentation to his company's investors. The CEO of the company confided in me that he was afraid turning the vice president loose on the investors could be a damaging decision. Frankly, at the beginning of our first session, I began to feel as though the CEO were right. The executive stumbled his way through the entire presentation, not knowing how to start, when to end, or where to look. Another person in the organization told me that hundreds of employees were losing confidence in this person. We had to work fast to save his reputation, his job, and his company's future.

Fortunately, it was an easy fix. Once he rehearsed his opening hook, once he knew exactly the point he needed to drive home with each slide, and once he could take his eyes off the slides and focus on his audience, the vice president came off as a fine communicator. In fact, one of the most gratifying points in my coaching career occurred when I returned to the company for a follow-up. A secretary in the company rushed up to me to say that she now considered this vice president a "real leader" whereas she was losing faith in him before our coaching sessions. In this case, preparation literally saved a company and a career.

★ ★ ★

Matt Eversmann is a military hero immortalized in the book and movie *Black Hawk Down*. I had the pleasure of striking up a friendship with him at a business conference. Not once during his twenty-minute talk did he stand behind the podium. He faced his audience the whole time. When I asked him how he did it he responded, "I spent a month rehearsing!" Eversmann says he doesn't like listening to people who look down the whole time they speak. You might as well shoot yourself in the foot if you shoot off the cuff.

If You Look at the Map Too Long You'll Drive off the Road

Reciting facts, figures, and statistics is nearly impossible for most of us to do without looking down at notes or slides. It's perfectly acceptable to glance away from the audience every now and then. But your opener, your closer, and 90 percent of everything in between should be delivered by looking directly into the eyes of your audience. In this case, PowerPoint slides or notecards can be your single greatest ally because they serve as your outline or guide. Use the title of the slide and the bullet points to jog your memory. It'll make you appear far more relaxed, spontaneous, and confident.

Above all—don't read. That's why television anchors use teleprompters, so they can look directly at their viewers. In fact, although the words scroll in front of them (they can see the words, you can't), the best anchors in the business are those who don't appear as though they're reading. Whenever I do a story in the field, without the benefit of a teleprompter, I'm always careful to commit my opening and closing line to memory. Next time you watch the news, see what happens the minute the reporter looks down at their notes—they'll lose your attention. Unfortunately, most presenters will spend the majority of their time reading from slides or notes instead of using those notes solely as guideposts.

Stuart Varney told me "under no circumstances do I read a script. I never, ever, have a speech printed out that I read to the audience. I feel very, very strongly that it does not work in terms of communicating. Any audience knows when it's being read to. It lacks vitality, dynamism. It's not a good way of communicating." It certainly isn't. Read and much of your credibility as a speaker will fly away like a lost kite—nearly impossible to retrieve.

★ ★ ★

"The less you refer to notes, the more you make that indispensable eye contact, the first source of rapport with your audience."
Jack Valenti, President of the Motion Picture Association of America, in *Speak Up with Confidence*

Get Caught on Tape

Rehearsing should be an important part of your preparation routine and that includes seeing yourself on video. Video cameras are inexpensive and will make up for their cost many times over in the success you enjoy as a presenter. When I begin to work with clients, most have rarely, if ever, seen their presentations on video. But when they do, it's an eye-opener. Watching yourself is an easy way to get rid of visual or audible distractions like poor eye contact, irritating gestures, bad posture, or annoying habits like using too many "ums" and "ahs" when you talk. You'll be in a better position to objectively evaluate your performance on videotape after you finish identifying and adopting all 10 Simple Secrets, but I've added some simple things to watch for in the Coaching Drills at the end of this chapter.

"Practice, practice, practice," says CEO comic David Moore. Yes, you read that correctly, "CEO comic." Moore is chairman of the New York venture capital firm Sonostar Ventures. He's a Harvard MBA who starts companies and invests in promising startups. That's his day job. By night, he's a stand-up comic! No joke. He's headlined Caroline's on Broadway and the Improve in Los Angeles. How's that for a unique resumé?

"Not every executive can, or should, do stand-up on their off time," I told Moore. "So what can they do to improve their skills as presenters?" I asked.

"Good stand-up is 50 percent material and 50 percent presentation," Moore said.

I think the same goes for business information. The material needs to be well written, concise, interesting, and compelling. But it also needs to be presented in an interesting manner. Don't ignore either. And practice, practice, practice. In front of a mirror, in front of a colleague. I think it's a mistake to make an important presentation without at least one practice session. Jerry Seinfeld, in his movie *The Comedian,* showed the world that he needs dozens of times on stage to perfect the presentation of one joke. And he is one of the greatest stand-up comedians of all time. No business person should treat an important presentation any differently. Good preparation and lots of practice will ensure the right message lands clearly.

I think Moore would appreciate my reference to Harvard. As he says in his act, "I went to Harvard Business School. I only mention that because as Harvard alumni we're required to work it into the first two minutes of any conversation."

The Pastry Won't Puff If the Oven Isn't Hot

Preparation is vital to establishing rapport with your audience—getting 'em to care about you and your message. Prepare by mastering your material: knowing your audience and rehearsing your presentation. By doing so, you make yourself the visual. PowerPoint slides, handouts, or other types of multimedia should only serve to compliment your presentation, but the audience wants to hear from you. Stuart Varney says that speaking is a form of entertainment. Yes, your audience wants to learn information but they also don't want to be bored. Varney wants the audience to be wrapped up in him and his message, not on the slides, notes, or handouts. That's why he's so well prepared—so he can build a relationship directly with his listeners. Varney tosses the script! So should you. Don't read from prepared notes. It'll separate you from your competition and eliminate the separation between you and your listeners.

Great presenters prepare for their roles just as great athletes prepare for competition. Swedish golf sensation Annika Sorenstam is said to be more prepared than anyone on the Ladies Professional Golf Association tour. She practices every detail of every shot. She prepares so meticulously that nothing surprises her during a tournament. Sorenstam has "internalized" the game so she doesn't have to worry about mechanics on the course. Once you've prepared and practiced for your presentation, you'll have internalized the content in much the same way, freeing yourself to focus on the audience and not on the mechanics of your talk. You'll use notes or slides only to jog your memory. You'll talk to your audience, not at your slide show. You'll make your listeners feel more connected to you and your message. Preparing and rehearsing is the only way to do it.

Look, you don't have to take this advice. Go ahead, continue to wing it. But rest assured; you'll have competitors who prepare for their presentations, meetings, or interviews. You might even have a better product to pitch! I don't want you to miss an opportunity because you failed to prepare. You're on your way to becoming a winning presenter—start rehearsing for the role!

Your audience won't follow you until they like you, until you take the initiative to build a relationship with them. Only then will they be receptive to your message. Once you've gotten your audience to care about your message by being passionate, inspirational, and prepared, it's time to grab 'em and keep 'em by identifying the next three Simple Secrets of great communicators.

★ COACHING DRILLS ★

1. **Watch a Master in Action.** Visit www.carminegallo.com for video links to a John Chambers presentation. Ask yourself the following questions:

- How does Chambers keep the attention focused on himself and the message?

_____

_____

_____

_____

_____

- How often does Chambers read from the slides?

_____

_____

_____

_____

_____

- What else about this presentation reflects Chambers intense preparation?

_____

_____

_____

_____

_____

2. **Get to Know Your Audience.** Answer the following questions about your audience prior to your next presentation:

- What do they need to know?

_____

_____

• Why should they care?

_____

_____

_____

_____

_____

• What action do I want them to take?

_____

_____

_____

_____

_____

3. **See Yourself on Video.** Videotape your presentation and watch it. Use an external, clip-on microphone instead of the microphone built-in to the camera. Your voice will sound louder, clearer, and more resonant, which will help to pick up on vocal weaknesses. If possible, find objective friends or colleagues who will give you honest feedback. If I were watching your video, here's what I would look for:

• Ask yourself—does this person engage me? Do I want to hear more? Is she/he convincing? Genuine? Passionate? (Simple Secret #1)
• How's your energy level? You might feel as though you're enthusiastic about the topic but the video doesn't lie—it will show whether you look like you've just rolled out of bed on a Sunday morning or if you're truly engaged, enthusiastic, and electrifying! (Simple Secrets #1 & #9)
• Do you get to the point quickly or do you tend to meander from thought to thought? Is your message clear or convoluted? (Simple Secrets #5 & #6)
• What does your body language say? Do you exude strong, confident,

and commanding body language? Are your arms crossed instead of open? Do you fidget, rock, or have other distracting body mannerisms? If so, the videotape will help you identify bad habits and eliminate them. (Simple Secret #8)

- Do you use comfortable, animated, and purposeful hand gestures or do you look stiff and wooden? (Simple Secret #8)
- Do you have nonsense or filler words that you repeat all the time while you're thinking? For example, one client of mine would say "okay?" after virtually every sentence. He easily caught himself using the word on video and immediately ended the annoying habit. (Simple Secret #7)
- How do you look? Is your wardrobe disheveled or crisp? Do the colors you wear compliment your skin tone or do you look washed out? Do you look a little better than the people in your audience? (Simple Secret #9)

NOTES:

_____

_____

_____

_____

_____

PART TWO

Once you've built rapport with your audience, they'll be receptive to your message. But now what? You've got to grab 'em, keep 'em interested, and, most importantly, get them to take a desired action—whether it's to use your service, buy your product, invest in your company, or support your cause.

The great business communicators who reveal their secrets in this section will teach you how to:

- Captivate your audience in the first few seconds
- Articulate a crystal-clear message anyone can understand
- Earn a reputation for being a spokesman who is not only clear but concise

Grabbing and keeping your audience's attention requires that you start strong, end strong, make it clear, and keep it brief. So here we go—Simple Secret #4!

SIMPLE SECRET #4: START STRONG

DON'T BURY THE LEAD

"A powerful beginning and end will stick with your listeners."

Monster Worldwide

"I want an open and candid discussion from everyone in my group. I don't want a few brave people to speak, but everyone."

MONSTER FOUNDER JEFF TAYLOR

Jeff Taylor has reinvented the way millions of people look for jobs. Before Taylor founded Monster in 1994, looking for a new job meant getting gobs of black ink on your fingers as you skimmed the classified ads in the newspaper. Monster is a rare Internet success story. Monster made a big splash with its quirky 1999 Super Bowl ads showing kids expressing less than audacious goals such as, "When I grow up I want to file all day" or, "...become a yes man" or, "...have a brown nose." Since those first ads, Monster has become as synonymous with online job hunting as Amazon has with books or eBay with auctions.

As Chief Monster—yes that's his real title—Taylor gives anywhere from thirty-five to seventy speeches a year. His topics range from entrepreneurship to employment. He's always captivating, consistently inspiring, and constantly promoting the Monster brand. "I feel as the CEO, you always have to put yourself out in front of the brand," Taylor told me during one of our long conversations about his presentation style.

The world's greatest business communicators start strong. It's the secret behind grabbing your listeners and keeping their attention focused on you and your message.

Taylor understands the power of a strong opener. In a commencement address to the University of Massachusetts graduating class of 2001, Taylor had thirty thousand people in the stadium completely mesmerized. With the flair of a television evangelist, he had the crowd repeating phrases in unison on his command. Here's a brief transcript from the first couple of minutes of his speech:

> [Taylor] I've got some words that I'm going to say and I want you to give me some words back, can we do that?
> [cheers]
> All right, my first word when I talk about the future, I want you to say, "I believe." Can you do that?
> No shit, you're actually gonna do this right now, all right.
> [laughter]
> All right, we're gonna talk about the future and you're gonna say,
> [Audience] I believe!
> [Taylor] I know you can be louder than that so I'm gonna talk about the future and you're gonna say,
> [Audience] I believe!
> [Taylor] All right, I'm gonna talk about UMass. When I say UMass I want you to say, "We rock." Can you do that?
> [cheers]
> So I'm gonna talk about UMass and you're gonna say,
> [Audience] We rock!
> [Taylor] I can't hear you!
> [Audience] We rock!

Taylor kept this up for several minutes, getting the crowd to repeat phrases like "Hallelujah," "I believe," and "We rock!" Hallelujah!

How to Get Five Hundred People to Take Off Their Shoes

It's easy to see why Taylor is one of the most captivating speakers in the business world. To my knowledge, he's not a Lutheran minister, but he sure sounds like one. Taylor doesn't save these openings just for commencement addresses. Speaking to a group of human resources professionals in Chicago, he had them chanting just like the UMass graduates. When Taylor said "Chicago HR," the audience would yell back, "We rock!"

"Why do you kick off your presentations by getting the audience to repeat phrases like 'We rock,' or 'We believe'?" I asked Taylor.

"I do it because if I'm going to speak to my audience for an hour, I want an open and candid discussion from everyone in my group. I don't want a few brave people to speak, but everyone. For example," Taylor continued,

> In my talks about innovation, I begin by asking people if they are innovators. Then I take off my shoe and invite people to hold their shoes in the air. Then I point out the true innovators—the early adopters—the massive middle, and the shoe laggards. I get a room of five hundred people to take off their shoes. Then I interview the shoe innovator (first person) and have a frank discussion with laggards who never joined the party.

Taylor grabs his audience's attention and holds them by making his presentation and its message memorable. The more memorable the message, the easier it is to act upon. Don't get me wrong—I am not suggesting you act like a rock star before your next budget presentation. In fact, I'm quite confident that if you tried to pull off the same thing that Taylor does, you may hear those words that Donald Trump made famous on *The Apprentice*—"You're fired!" Taylor has a lot of experience; he speaks before crowds of several thousands, and his audiences expect him to be a little outrageous, to push the envelope. They don't expect it from you. But they do expect you to grab their attention.

The Apple and the Pomegranate

In *Selling the Invisible,* marketing expert Harry Beckwith writes about a study that reinforces the theme of this chapter. When people are shown a series of objects for a few seconds, say a group of fruits like an apple, pear, peach, plum, and pomegranate, what are they most likely to remember? The first and last items on the list—the apple and the pomegranate. I'll bet you never knew fruit could teach you this much! The "fruit lesson" applies to presentations as well (A pomegranate is a fruit, isn't it? If not, my apologies to the fruit family). People tend to remember the first thing you say and the last.

We know that first impressions are made quickly, and they last. How quickly? Who really knows? I've heard that listeners form their impressions of a speaker in the first thirty seconds, ninety seconds, even the first two seconds! It's fast. Let's leave it at that.

Don't Bury the Lead

In journalism, when the headline of a story is buried somewhere in the middle of it, we call it "burying the lead." It's a no-no. The same is true when pitching, promoting, or presenting—if you're speaking for fifteen minutes on a particular subject and you wait fourteen minutes before announcing the headline, or key message, of your topic, you've already lost your listeners. In fact, they probably started looking at their watches long ago.

Apple Computers CEO Steve Jobs is a masterful communicator, one of the most compelling business speakers of our time. He always starts strong. Jobs kicks off his presentations with exactly what the audience wants to hear. He never buries the lead.

When thousands of Apple employees, analysts, and investors gathered at San Francisco's Moscone Center to hear Jobs introduce a new music service for Windows users, Apple's portable music player, the iPod, was the hottest consumer electronics product of the season. Gadget lovers were snapping up iPods at the rate of two units per minute. The iPod had to be the "lead" of the presentation and Jobs knew it. Here's how he began:

> We're here to talk about music, so let's get started. The first thing we want to talk about is the iPod. The iPod is amazing. These new third generation iPods are as thin as two CD jewel cases back to back. And they have a dock which makes it even easier to charge them and sync them with your Mac. They're fantastic products. We started with one thousand songs in your pocket. Now we're up to ten thousand songs in your pocket, an amazing product. Today we have some new features to announce to make it even better.

Jobs spent all of two minutes and six seconds to get his audience pumped up about the success of Apple's hottest product. He didn't bury the lead. In fact, Jobs always kicks off his presentations with what he knows his audience is there to hear.

The next day a newspaper reporter wrote that Jobs always puts on a "fabulous" show. Yes he does. I want you to do the same. Put on a fabulous show by captivating your listeners from the start.

Watch Us Now!

Before resigning as Hewlett Packard's CEO on February 9, 2005, Carly Fiorina spent six years at the helm of the giant computer company. In September of 2001, Fiorina led one of the most ambitious and contentious marriages in corporate history—HP's $19 billion merger with Compaq. She had her work cut out for her. A powerful board member and son of one of the company's founders, Walter Hewlett, opposed the merger. Fiorina had to convince analysts, customers, the press, large shareholders, and nearly one hundred fifty thousand employees that the merger made sense. She pulled it off brilliantly. In an article shortly after the merger, *Fortune* magazine praised Fiorina for her persuasive presentations. "By the end of the hour, she had this crowd of six thousand sophisticated tech buyers eating out of her hand," wrote reporter Adam Lashinsky.

In October of 2000, when *Fortune* named Fiorina the most powerful woman in business, Fiorina talked about the importance of communication skills to her role as a leader. "A company is people—people with brains and hearts and guts. If you're a leader, you've got to capture the whole person. People want to see you get it intellectually and feel it emotionally," said Fiorina.

Fiorina has been able to capture an emotional spirit and share it with her audience for most of her career. As a top executive at Lucent in 1995, Fiorina was involved in the company's spin-off from AT&T. Her mission was to prepare financial documents and to stir up investor excitement in the new stock. In *Perfect Enough, Carly Fiorina and the Reinvention of Hewlett Packard,* George Anders quotes Lucent investment banker Jeff Williams who recalled, "We had a good story and we told it perfectly…give Carly all the credit for making it happen."

Anders describes how Fiorina "enchanted" crowds with her wardrobe (Simple Secret #9), her body language (Simple Secret #7), and her "intoxicatingly appealing version of the future" (Simple Secret #2). According to Anders, "the full power of her remarks came at the end, when she let go of everything except her own faith. Her final three words in New York, 'Watch us now!' brought some investors to their feet." Professional investors rarely give standing ovations. You've really got to grab 'em to make it happen. Fiorina did because she sparkles. I know you can, too.

Fiorina understands the power of Simple Secret #4. She always begins her presentations with a punch and makes sure her opening remarks tie in to the central theme of her talk. Fiorina started her keynote at the 2002 Comdex (a giant computer show in Las Vegas) by taking the stage after the audience saw a new HP television ad. She said:

Good morning.

What you just saw is an ad that will begin running this morning.

We call this ad Anthem.

It's part of a campaign that will feature the stories of our customers and how they use our technology.

And all of these customers that we will feature have one thing in common.

Every one of them was told that what they hoped to accomplish was impossible.

FedEx was told they'd never make an overnight delivery service work.

Amazon was told they'd never make online retailing work.

BMW's Formula One team was told they'd never make a car that rivals Ferrari.

In every single case, they proved the skeptics wrong.

And in every single case, HP was there.

Why is this the face we have chosen to show the world?

Because it's about everything we can achieve, working together.

It's an affirmation of our belief that progress is not made by the cynics and the doubters, it is made by those who believe that everything is possible.

That got my attention. Fiorina even maintains the consistency between what she says and HP's advertising campaign at the same time, "Everything is possible." She ended the speech by returning to the same towering vision and to the central theme:

At HP, the idea that we can help make more things more possible for more people in more places represents our highest aspirations— as well as our most practical goals as a company and as a partner. It is at the intersection of practice and promise that you will find today's HP. Progress is not made by the cynics or the doubters; progress is made by those who believe everything is possible.

Great communicators like Fiorina know the secret to grabbing 'em and keeping 'em is to get their attention from the start. Don't bury the lead. Begin with a bang and explode at the end.

The Thirty-Second Lead

When journalists introduce a story, it's called The Lead. In television, it's typically no longer than fifteen to thirty seconds. It's meant to be so intriguing that you'll want to hear the rest of the story. If all the leads are interesting, you'll stick with the entire newscast. If you watch the whole news program, you'll keep advertisers happy. Happy advertisers keep the staff happy because they retain their jobs, get raises, and if all goes well, they get to attend an awesome holiday party at the Four Seasons instead of Tico's Tacos. And to think it all starts with a great lead!

The easiest way to develop a strong opening for your next presentation, talk, workshop, or meeting is simply to create a compelling lead that you can say in thirty seconds. If you can say it in twenty seconds, even better. The lead should be a short description of your service, product, company, or cause that your grandmother could understand. It must be clear, concise, and compelling. The world's greatest business communicators have their leads down cold. You can, too.

Good Lead; Bad Hair

While I was writing this book, I was glued to the first season of Donald Trump's reality show, *The Apprentice*. Billed as the ultimate job interview, sixteen young entrepreneurs vie for a $250,000-a-year job with Trump's company. The show was a guilty sort of pleasure, giving you a glimpse of The Donald's world for an hour a week. It was good television (*The Apprentice* averaged twenty-two million viewers). I was struck by the scenes in the boardroom at the end of each episode. Trump would grill the losing team, point a finger at someone, and say those two simple words, "You're fired!"

After watching several interviews with Trump during the show's first season, I really started to like the guy's presentation skills. I think he's mastered most, if not all, of the 10 Simple Secrets. No kidding. Look, I know Trump has an ego—but he's the first to admit it.

Trump can get away with the things he says because he has a track record to back it up. When he says his new golf course in Los Angeles will put Pebble Beach to shame, he has a reputation for building unbelievable properties. If you claim the company you're starting from your bedroom will put IBM to shame, you'll be laughed out of the room. You've been warned. Now let's talk about Trump and the lead. Trump has a lead for every project—a property, golf course, or television show—just about anything he's asked about!

During an interview with CNN's Larry King on April 27, 2004, Trump said,

> I'm the biggest developer in New York, by far. There's nobody close. I'm building buildings all over the place. I'm building a big building in Chicago, one of the largest buildings built in Chicago—the largest building since the Sears Tower. In Los Angeles now, I'm doing a big development in Palos Verdes, a big golf course which will hopefully put Pebble Beach to shame. It's two miles along the Pacific Ocean, three hundred acres. It's going to be amazing.

When asked to describe the success of *The Apprentice*, Trump said, "Well, I think it's something that people want. It's *Survivor*, but it's the real survivor. It's in the jungle of New York. People can relate to the New York, and that's really what they want....Last night, we were number one in demographics. And that's the important rating, as you know, the eighteen to forty-nine age group." Trump boasts about his show or his properties but he backs it with facts. He differentiates his properties and his show. He makes you want to hear more. He may have mastered the art of the deal, but he's also mastered the lead.

★ ★ ★

Eight wannabe Donald Trumps auditioned for a chance to be one of the finalists for the second season of the show, *The Apprentice 2*. Thousands of people auditioned at casting calls around the country. On NBC's *Today Show,* producers gave each of the eight candidates thirty seconds to pitch themselves. Most failed miserably. With Trump sitting across from them, anchor Matt Lauer asked each one a slightly different version of the same question, "Why do you want to work for Trump?" Only three of eight contestants answered the first key question of a great lead— what do you do? We learned one was a lawyer and the other owned a company in New York's fashion district. The others used empty phrases like: I have talents, I'm a strategy thinker, I love to learn, etc. Trump had to interrupt several people to ask what they did for a living.

Most also failed to answer the question, "How are you different?" One had an MBA. With a record number of students graduating with MBAs, simply having the degree isn't enough to differentiate yourself. Trump wasn't impressed. Most of the candidates crashed and burned by failing to answer the key question, "Why should you care?" In this case, Trump wants to make money. Period. And he wants someone to run one of his companies who will help him make more of it. The candidates would say things like, "I started twenty years ago with nothing but a phone and a telephone book and today, twenty years later, I have one thousand clients." Sounds good. But Trump had to ask what the candidate did and how he could help Trump International. One young woman said she had worked herself up from receptionist to owning her own company. Again, Trump was forced to ask, "And what are you going to do for me?"

Take the Lead

Whether you're a mogul or an apprentice, take the lead in your presentations. Tory Johnson is the founder and CEO of Women for Hire, the world's largest career fair for women. Her organization puts on twenty events per year to connect female job seekers and employers. After interviewing Johnson, I learned that she's a big believer in the thirty-second pitch, which she considers the ideal amount of time to "toot your own horn." Johnson says there isn't a big difference between thirty seconds and one minute, but thirty seconds is a good time to keep in the back of your head. Any longer gives you too much room to ramble. The content of your pitch is more important than being obsessed with the time, says Johnson. I couldn't agree more. But where Trump has no problem promoting himself, Johnson says many women have the opposite problem: they minimize their accomplishments.

Johnson offers this advice to readers of *10 Simple Secrets of the World's Greatest Business Communicators*:

> Never belittle your role. So many times in conversation, job candidates will say things like "I just do the bookkeeping," or, "I only have a few years of experience." When you undersell your value and achievements, it takes away from who you are and what you offer. If you undervalue or belittle who you are or the work you've performed, there's a good chance someone else will undervalue it as well. You always want to come across as someone who is comfortable, confident, and proud of his or her achievements.

Johnson says she often sees great titles, great companies, and great qualifications, but the job candidates who can quantify their success land the plum roles.

★ ★ ★

Women for Hire by Tory Johnson is a great book about how to sell yourself on the phone, at career fairs, at networking events, or in front of recruiters. Aimed at women, its advice applies to men as well. Johnson believes in the power of the thirty-second lead or pitch. She writes, "A poor, pathetic pitch—one that's delivered in a boring mon-otone manner and lacking any clear message—will surely result in a dead end." If you can't get people interested in you in the first thirty seconds, Johnson argues, they'll move on. Her book offers more than a dozen sample pitches for a variety of careers from accounting and aerospace to lawyer, secretary, or teacher. Check it out!

Tory Johnson's Thirty-Second Pitch Tips

"Tory, if you only have thirty seconds to sell yourself, what would you consider the elements of a great pitch?" I asked Johnson. She gave me these three tips:

1. First and foremost, state your name! Women, more so than men, have a challenge because we want to err on the friendly side. I'm not Oprah or Madonna. I'm not on a first name basis with the world. Always present yourself in a business situation with your first and last name. Beyond that, I want to tell you who I am and what I offer.

2. Secondly, when describing your accomplishments, remember that numbers count. Quantify something. For example, there's a big differ-ence between saying "I'm in Human Resources" or "I'm a Human Resource manager with experience at *Fortune* 500 companies." That's quantifying. Include impressive details. They get people's attention. Better yet—"I've worked in Human Resources for *Fortune* 500 compa-nies for the past ten years and I've hired over one hundred people." Focus on accomplishments, not responsibilities.

3. Finally, rehearse your pitch so it comes off naturally, not like a patented pitch. Don't make it sound like you're reading it. Record it on a videocamera. Look for nuances. Do you avert your eyes? Do you use filler words like "um" and "ah"? You'll find things you cringe at. By taking steps to improve your performance, you'll come across as more confident and as someone others want to get to know.

Crafting Your Thirty-Second Lead

Johnson's advice applies to both men and women, whether you're looking for a new job, a better job, or a bigger office. Johnson's advice will help you get ahead. Now let's get started crafting a thirty-second lead you can call your own—whether you're pitching a service, product, company, cause, or yourself! After interviewing more than two thousand executives and spokespeople in my career, I'm convinced the best stand out by crafting a lead that answers the following four questions in thirty seconds or less:

1. What is my service, product, company, or cause?
2. What problem do I solve (or what demand do I meet)?
3. How am I different?
4. Why should you care?

Answering these questions will help you start strong while giving the rest of your presentation a direction. During a corporate workshop in Monterey, California, I worked with a group of executives on the company's opening pitch. After about an hour of brainstorming, we came up with a powerful thirty-second pitch—but only after answering the four questions. Let me start with the result:

Language Line Services is the world's largest provider of phone interpretation services for companies who want to connect with their non-English speaking customers. Every twenty-three seconds, someone who doesn't speak English enters the country. When they call a hospital, a bank, an insurance company, or 911, it's likely that a Language Line interpreter is on the other end. We help you talk to your customers, patients, or sales prospects in one hundred fifty languages!

This takes less than thirty seconds to say and gives potential customers a reason to learn more about the company. Watch how simple it was to put this example together after answering the four questions:

Question 1: What is my service, product, company or cause? "Language Line is the world's largest provider of phone interpretation services." If your company doesn't offer a tangible product, but a service, say so.

Question 2: What problem do I solve? "Every twenty-three seconds, someone who doesn't speak English enters the country." Every service, product, company, or cause must solve a problem or satisfy a demand that's being unmet. Otherwise, you might as well be making buggy whips in the automobile age.

Question 3: How am I different? "When you call a hospital, a bank, an insurance company, or 911, it's likely that a Language Line interpreter is on the other end." By not directly saying "we're number one in the industry," the pitch takes a softer approach but still lets the potential customer know that the company is a leader in its field. Odds are, you're not the only one doing what you're doing. Be different.

Question 4: Why should you care? "We help you talk to your customers, patients, or sales prospects in one hundred fifty languages." Wow! Now I want to hear more. If you can't tell your audience why your product or service will improve their lives (or their financial well-being), they will dismiss you faster than movie audiences tuned out *Gigli*.

It's that simple to start strong. Answer those four questions and you'll stand out. Your listeners just want to know, in a clear and concise pitch, what you do, what problem you solve, how you're different, and why they should care about you or your message.

As a former managing director for the investment bank Robertson Stephens, Rick Juarez saw ten to fifteen presentations a week in addition to taking more than fifteen companies public. Today he continues to evaluate business plans and presentations as founder of his own financial advisory and venture firm, AlphaCap Ventures. Juarez tells me the number one pitfall for most corporate speakers is failing to help the audience see the difference between their product and those of their competitors. Is your product or service "cheaper" than existing solutions? Than say so. Is it "better"? Than tell me why. Is it "faster"? Then prove it! According to Juarez, clearly stating what your product or service is, how it fits in your audience's needs, and how it's different from anything currently available will help the listener determine whether your product or service is a "must have" or simply "nice to have."

Chamber of Commerce Catastrophe

While writing this chapter, I attended a chamber of commerce luncheon in which a local firm was featured as the company of the month. The chamber's executive director read a description of the company from its website—hardly a stirring introduction that showed no personal touch. Nothing new, I thought. This is the same scenario repeated in thousands of meetings around the world every day. At least the CEO of the featured company had a platform to pitch his company. He would surely dazzle the crowd, wouldn't he? As is often the case, the CEO fell flatter than a Ray's New York style pizza.

On this particular day, the CEO first thanked the group and proceeded to "pitch" his company. He said his company provides web design and hosting, and if anyone in the group needed help, call or visit the website. That's it. I'm not kidding. Not a word more. He didn't seem nervous, he just hadn't mastered this Simple Secret. He blew an opportunity to start strong and end with a call to action.

A quick Google search will turn up 5.5 million sites under the term "web design and hosting." Everyone does it. What made this guy's company any different? Get this—I only learned at the end of the luncheon that this particular firm designed the chamber's website and won an award for it! Look, you don't have to boast like Donald Trump, but c'mon, give me a little something. Imagine if this particular CEO had mastered his thirty-second lead by saying:

"Thank you for making my company, XYZ, the featured firm of the month. It's especially timely this month as we helped the chamber of commerce boost its membership. We work with local companies to improve their sales by designing more effective websites [What is our service]. Every business needs a website if it's to be taken seriously, but research shows that the vast majority of websites fail to improve business as much as they should. Our clients have a different experience [What demand we meet]. We design and host more local websites than any other firm. In fact, most of you are familiar with the chamber's website that we designed. We're proud to say it has won an award as the best chamber of commerce website on the West Coast! [How we're different]. But we're not in this to win awards. We're in it to make our clients money. On average, our clients find that sales soar 25 percent within two weeks of launching their website [why should you care]."

Okay, so it might take a little longer than thirty seconds to say. Maybe forty seconds. But you get the point. It's clear, concise, and compelling. A lead like this will grab the audience's attention, keep them interested and possibly get their business.

> ★ ★ ★
>
> "We try to communicate like a good novel. There has to be some moment when you say to yourself, 'Now I care about what the speaker has to say.' We start with the answer then explain why. That's how we communicate as a company. It reflects our confidence in our opinion of the world."
>
> Ron Ricci, Vice President of Corporate Positioning, Cisco Systems

Jerry Seinfeld Had It Right: Go Out on Top

The flip side of starting strong is ending strong. Go out on top. *Friends* and *Frasier* overstayed their welcome but *Seinfeld* went off the air at its peak (you wouldn't know it by the last episode, but who's quibbling). The world's greatest business communicators always end their presentations by leaving the audience with something memorable—usually, but not always, with a call to action.

Remember at the beginning of this chapter how Steve Jobs introduced the new iPod? At the end of that particular presentation, he tried to touch the heart of his audience as well as stir them to action. Here's how he closed it:

> I just want to end by saying, we are very lucky. We love doing what we do. And we work really hard at it because we love it. And I want to thank...all the great folks at Apple who brought this to you today. We love what we do so much. I also want to thank the families, the spouses, the girlfriends, the boyfriends, the partners, that let us do this thing we love. Because without this support, we couldn't do it. Please go out and try this stuff out for yourself. Thank you very much.

Jobs had just spent the better part of the presentation making an emotional connection with his audience by showing them all the cool things they could do with the new iPod. He even had singer/songwriter Sarah McLachlan perform at the end of the presentation. Jobs is a showman. He also has a lot of money. You're not going to get McLachlan to sing at your next staff meeting. Your budget may not allow it. Vanilla Ice, maybe. But the point is that by starting strong and ending on a heartfelt note about how much his employees love what they do, Jobs touched his audience, got them to share the excitement, and then, at his peak, asked them to try it for themselves. Who can resist? After all, the folks who make the iPod love what they do. Jobs said so. By gosh, they even appreciate their families for giving them the opportunity to do what they love. I'm being a bit sarcastic but you know what I'm getting at. Jobs doesn't miss a chance to pitch the product once he gets his audience to buy into the message. I don't have statistics, but I'm willing to bet a lot of iPods were sold after that presentation.

Leave 'Em Wanting More

The organizer of the legendary Bakersfield Business Conference, George Martin, has invited the world's greatest speakers to address his audiences year after year. Famous actors, influential politicians, powerful world leaders. They've all been there. When I asked Martin how the best of the best structure their presentations, he said: "Carmine, they know what they're going to say, how they're going to say it, and how they're going to hit their ending…they always end on an inspiring note. When you're finished, you want to leave the audience wanting more. No matter how great you are or how much you've accomplished, you don't want the audience to say to themselves, 'When is this person going to stop?' Don't drag out your talk. Know how you're going to end."

Wimps Don't Make Good Leaders

Great endings don't always have to include a call to action. I once read that "wimps don't make good leaders." It's true. As we discussed in chapter 2, audiences love bold, optimistic language. It reminds me of National Semiconductor CEO Brian Halla, who closed his 2002 Comdex keynote speech with a bold prediction. At the time of his speech, Silicon Valley was going through the worst economic downturn in half a century. Halla ended his presentation by predicting the exact date of the economic recovery, June 21, 2003. Of course some of it was tongue-in-cheek, as nobody with the exception of Nostradamus could predict that event. Did Halla turn out to be right? I'm not exactly sure. The economy did start to improve but did he accurately pinpoint the date? Who cares. That's beside the point. Halla was the talk of the convention. His "prediction" made headlines the next day. His company's name was on everyone's lips for the rest of the week. I remember the bold prediction at the end of his presentation. As for the rest of his speech? I'm sure he said some interesting things as he usually does. He's a brilliant CEO. But heck if I remember it.

Your listeners will remember your apple and your pomegranate—the way you start your presentation and the way you end it. Grab their attention at the beginning and leave them wanting more at the end. That's the way to stand out. That's the way to be remembered!

Now that you've grabbed your listener's attention and they want to hear more, it's time to make sure your message is heard by revealing the fifth Simple Secret of the world's greatest business communicators.

★ COACHING DRILLS ★

1. **Craft Your Thirty-Second Lead.** Answer the following questions:

• What is my service, product, company, or cause?

_____

_____

_____

_____

_____

• What problem do I solve?

_____

_____

_____

_____

_____

• How am I different?

_____

_____

_____

_____

_____

• Why should you care?

_____

_____

_____

_____

_____

2. **Time Yourself.** Use a stopwatch to time yourself. You should be able to deliver your lead in thirty seconds or less. Sixty seconds won't hurt, but it's a good discipline to keep it shorter.

SIMPLE SECRET #5: CLARITY

LOSE THE JARGON OR LOSE YOUR AUDIENCE

"Insecure managers create complexity. Real leaders don't need clutter."

JACK WELCH

Justin Sullivan/Getty Images

"Do you want to sell sugared water all your life or do you want to change the world?"

APPLE COMPUTERS CEO STEVE JOBS TO
FORMER PEPSI CEO JOHN SCULLEY

The movie *Black Hawk Down* captures the heroic struggle of 119 U.S. soldiers caught in a harrowing battle with ten thousand enemy fighters during a mission in Mogadishu, Somalia on October 3, 1993. It's an inspiring movie, portraying the discipline, courage, and loyalty of elite soldiers who live by a simple code—no one gets left behind.

I've had several conversations with the commander in charge of that mission, Sgt. Matt Eversmann. Effective communication is at the heart of his leadership course at Johns Hopkins University.

Military missions are extraordinarily complicated, requiring immense coordination, preparation, and rehearsal. But when communicating orders to ground forces, great military leaders keep it short, simple, and clear. For example, the operation in Somalia required seventeen helicopters that could only fly over certain areas of the city, twenty vehicles that could only drive in specific parts, and they all needed to be in precise coordination. According to Eversmann, in every mission each soldier knows his role but doesn't have to know all the moving pieces. It's the commander's job to cut the clutter. Eversmann's orders to his soldiers just before the Somalia mission could not have been simpler: "Surround the building, keep the bad guys out of our target area while our assault force does its stuff, and move out by air." Great leaders reinforce their messages…clearly.

★ ★ ★

Have you seen the movie *Master and Commander?* Russell Crowe plays Captain Jack Aubrey, commander of the HMS *Surprise.* I think it should be required viewing for MBA students who need a break from statistics for a lesson in leadership. Aubrey's ship has twenty-eight guns and nearly two hundred men. Facing the French enemy ship, *Acheron,* Aubrey realizes he's outgunned, outmanned, but not outsmarted. He comes up with a plan to disguise the ship as a damaged whaler. When the *Acheron* approaches, Aubrey raises the colors and springs the trap. Right before he implements the surprise attack, Aubrey gathers his men and uses a simple metaphor to inspire his men: "England is under threat of invasion. And though we be on the far side of the world, this ship is our home. This ship is England!"

Leaders on the front lines of any industry must strive for simplicity and clarity if they hope to inspire and motivate employees, customers or shareholders. During an interview for this book, Sybase CEO John Chen told me, "The single most important success factor for anybody in a leadership position is the ability to articulate a message passionately, concisely, and clearly." Chen says a big part of his job is to give presentations that cut through the complexity of the software industry for audiences made up of investors, customers, and employees. The world's greatest business communicators speak in clear terms everyone understands. Whether you're talking to your boss, a prospect, or colleagues, your listeners want to easily grasp the message behind your service, product, company, or cause. They want it clear and they want it fast.

SOC: Speaking of Confusion

Have you ever heard of a system-on-a-chip? Probably not, unless you're a technology journalist, work in the industry, or are an avid reader of technology trade journals targeting the semiconductor industry. But it's something that touches your life every day.

One of my clients, the CEO of a company in this particular industry, was struggling to describe his firm in clear, concrete, and concise language. His initial explanation failed to resonate with his audiences. The company's boilerplate description went like this: "Our company is a premier developer of intelligent semiconductor intellectual property solutions that dramatically accelerate complex SOC designs while minimizing risk." Not only is this explanation cluttered, convoluted, and confusing, it assumes that everyone knows what SOC means! Needless to say, we had our work cut out for us. We had to work fast to prepare this CEO for a major presentation to a group of semiconductor investors and analysts.

After about thirty minutes of grilling, the exasperated CEO finally blurted out, "Look Carmine, do you have a cell phone?"

"I sure do," I answered, anticipating a major breakthrough.

"Well, our technology makes cell phones that are smaller, more powerful, and last longer on a single charge," he said.

Wow, I thought. Now that makes it clear! The very next week, *Business Week* carried an entire article on the SOC industry titled "Dawn of the Superchip." The article explained that by adding more functions on a single computer chip, companies like my client's were creating cell phones that were cheaper, smaller, and could handle more features. Sound familiar? The message is clear, simple, and easy to understand.

★ ★ ★

Larry Page and Sergey Brin may have started their company during the dot-com mania, but never lost their penchant for straight talk. I recall interviewing the Google founders on TechTV and being struck by the simplicity of their business model and their presentation. When Google went public in 2004—making Page and Brin instant billionaires—it was clear the founders would continue to make history by creating a new kind of company that put employees, customers, and

> their long-term interests ahead of short-term forces. Page and Brin are contemporary communicators speaking to twenty-first-century audiences who are fed up with doublespeak. So the company's prospectus for potential investors put it plainly: "A management team distracted by a series of short-term targets is as pointless as a dieter stepping on a scale every half-hour."

Twenty-First-Century Communicators

If you're thinking to yourself, "That's great, Carmine, but our product is far too complicated to talk about in simple terms," you're wrong. That attitude will destroy your ability to connect with contemporary audiences. Albert Einstein once said nothing is so complex that it cannot be explained simply. He was right.

Look, if you're truly committed to transforming your audiences with your presentations, then you have no choice but to craft your message so everyone can grasp its implications. All the journalists I know hate confusing messages. They've been burned by dot-com marketing hype and they're skeptical of anything they can't understand quickly and easily. The same goes for most of your listeners. They're fed up with corporate speakers who are as murky as a Louisiana swamp in August.

After interviewing dozens of CEOs, executives, experts, and authors for this book, coaching hundreds through my seminars, and interviewing thousands of spokespeople in my television career, I strongly believe it's time for a new approach to executive communications—a twenty-first-century communicator who stresses simplicity without losing the substance of his or her message.

Clarity Can Make Your Stock Soar

"Today people place a strong premium on clarity," Reuters president Devin Wenig told me during one of our conversations for this book. "Shareholders will place more value on a company when they truly understand the risks and rewards of that company, its strategy and its management principles," says Wenig.

Wenig should know. The company's stock rose after one of Wenig's presentations was "well-received" according to newspapers. I've mentioned that during the writing of this book, Wenig was orchestrating a turnaround of Reuters, a 150-year-old media institution. It was critical for Wenig to articulate a clear direction.

> Reuters is a complex company that not a lot of people understand. Even our investors have trouble understanding Reuters. It's been a problem this company has had for many years. It's a very big company, it's a sprawling company. It's a news company but not exactly a news company. It's a technology company but not exactly a technology company. A financial services company but not exactly a financial services company. I think Reuters has suffered because people don't quite understand what the company is all about. When I speak in public forums about the company, my first goal is power and simplicity. I try to communicate the values and mission of the company simply, because at the end of the day it really is simple. You can make it complex or simple. There are certain core values about my company that need to be communicated very, very simply. After many years of being confused by Reuters, people are beginning to understand the company. And there is a strong premium to that clarity.

Great business communicators like Wenig use three techniques to make their messages clear:

1. They ask themselves, "Where's the Wow?"
2. They cut the jargon.
3. They dress up their message with story enhancers.

★ ★ ★

Top salespeople clearly and concisely communicate the benefit of their service, product, company, or cause to prospective customers. Will you be able to save your customers money? Make them money? Boost their productivity? Raise their visibility in the industry? If you can't answer these questions clearly for your prospects, you'll forever be stuck in the bottom 25 percent of sales professionals. To reach the top one percent you'll need to master all 10 Simple Secrets. So keep reading!

Where's the Wow?

Jack Welch is the one of the most admired and influential CEOs in the world. During his twenty years as GE's top executive, the conglomerate grew from $13 billion in revenue to $500 billion! Welch was on a mission to "de-clutter" everything about the company, from its management processes to its communication. He hated long and convoluted memos, meetings, and presentations.

In his book, *JACK: Straight from the Gut,* Welch discusses the initial meetings he had with division leaders that left him "underwhelmed." Clutter and jargon had no place in his meetings. If you wanted to upset the new CEO, just talk over his head. Welch would ask, "Let's pretend we're in high school...take me through the basics." Welch recalls his first meeting with one of his insurance leaders. Welch asked some simple questions about terms he was unfamiliar with. Welch writes, "So I interrupted him to ask: 'What's the difference between facultative and treaty insurance?' After fumbling through a long answer for several minutes, an answer I wasn't getting, he finally blurted out in exasperation, 'How do you expect me to teach you in five minutes what it has taken me twenty-five years to learn!' Needless to say, he didn't last long."

★ ★ ★

Welch had a clear and simple message for restructuring GE. Each division had to be first or second to its competition, otherwise it meant "fix, sell, or close." Welch said this approach "passed the simplicity test." Welch would ask himself, "If you're not already in the business, would you enter it today?" A simple question led to profound results.

Jeffrey Immelt took the reins of GE when Welch retired. He, too, strives to simplify the company's communications. *Fast Company* once featured Immelt's leadership tips that he teaches to executives at the company's famous management center at Crotonville. Immelt's ten leadership tips were titled "What Leaders Do." Number two on the list was SIMPLIFY CONSTANTLY. According to Immelt, "I always use Jack

[Welch] as my example here. Every leader needs to clearly explain the top three things the organization is working on. If you can't, then you're not leading well."

Immelt and Welch value clarity. Welch not only spoke simply, he expected the same from management presentations. It's been said that in meetings, Welch just wanted to know from his managers what had been the most exciting idea they had come up with the last ninety days. Instinctively, Welch knew to ask his managers what journalists are taught to ask themselves every time they sit down to write a story: Where's the Wow?

Finding the Wow

Journalists are trained to filter through the most complicated subjects to find the "Wow": the essence of the story that makes readers, viewers, or listeners perk up and pay attention. When I worked as a business correspondent for CNN, and later as a host and managing editor for TechTV, we would hold daily editorial meetings to discuss which stories were worth pursuing. As any journalist knows, the vast majority of press releases do little to help. Most are confusing, poorly written, or don't apply to a particular program.

During one particularly frustrating day at TechTV (Now G4, a video gaming television network) when we seemed to be rejecting every possible story idea, a senior producer wrote these three words on the board: Where's the Wow? It stuck. From that day on if a pitch didn't pass the Wow test, we would throw it out. The garbage couldn't be emptied fast enough. Whether your audience is made up of journalists, customers, or colleagues, everyone is looking for the Wow. Most corporate speakers could take some advice from journalists who are trained to find the Wow in the most confusing of stories. We'd rather be handed a clear story on a platter, but that's wishful thinking. It's as rare as a straight answer from a politician— it happens, but only on rare occasions. Corporate presenters who stand apart know that confusion is out. Clarity is in.

What You Encounter One Hundred Fifty Times a Day but Rarely See

Here's an example of a journalist turning a dull, convoluted message into a simple and exciting story. The following description is from the website of a company in Emeryville, California, called Wind River:

Wind River is the worldwide leader in embedded software and services. Wind River provides market-specific embedded platforms that integrate real-time operating systems, development tools, and technologies. Wind River's products and professional services are used in multiple markets including aerospace and defense, automotive, digital consumer, industrial, and network infrastructure. Wind River provides high-integrity technology and expertise that enables its customers to create superior products more efficiently.

Got it? Okay, tell me what this company does. I'm still waiting. Go ahead, read it again and tell me what they do. Actually, forget it. It won't make a difference. I've used this example in my workshops and to this day, I can't recall anyone who has been able to tell me exactly what this company does based on the information on its website. Oh, they've tried. Most have failed. I think one venture capitalist had an inkling, but couldn't quite clear it up for the rest of the group. And he invested in high-tech!

I bring up this example because one day at TechTV I interviewed the Wind River CEO (now former CEO). The company had just announced quarterly earnings and I was having a tough time explaining to others what the company produced and how it improved our lives. It was unclear to me. I couldn't answer the question at the editorial meeting, Where's the Wow? But the CEO had been booked for the show and I expected all my questions to be answered on the air. I'd pull a Larry King and ask basic questions my viewers would want to know, like what do you do and why should I care. It didn't work out as well as I had hoped. It was the longest live interview of my life. Unfortunately, I think the CEO wrote the description on the company's website!

Exactly one week after the CEO's appearance, I was on a Stairmaster reading a magazine called *Business 2.0.* Yes, I read on the Stairmaster, which means I'm not getting much of a workout but I sure learn a lot. Well, I read an article about a company that so captivated me, I couldn't wait to learn more about it—perhaps I could invite the CEO on our show, I thought. It was written by Paul Kaihla and titled "The Age of the Ubiqui-Chip." Here's how it started:

Riddle. What do you encounter one hundred fifty times a day and rarely, if ever, see? Here's a hint: it's something that Microsoft (MSFT) covets and chipmakers are wild about. Give up? Embedded systems. Simply put, an embedded system is just about anything with a microprocessor that's not a PC, server, or mainframe. It's the brain in your cell phone and your handheld computer, and it also controls such things as your refrigerator's cooling and defrost cycles. Your kid's Furby is on the list, as is one of Donald Rumsfeld's favorite war machines, the Tomahawk missile.

At this point, I was eager to learn more about the firms involved in this amazing industry. Imagine, these small computer systems that we don't see touch virtually every aspect of our lives. My viewers would love this! Much to my surprise, the article went on to say that about fifty companies are in this space but the unquestioned leader, with 40 percent of the market share is—you guessed it—Wind River! I almost fell off the exercise machine. There was the WOW I was looking for! Now why couldn't the CEO make it that clear?

If you've never read an issue of *Business 2.0,* you owe it to yourself to do so. This monthly magazine with a circulation of about six hundred thousand targets executives who are interested in business, technology, and innovation. Owned by Time-Warner, the magazine attracts some of the best writers in the industry who profile companies and individuals that integrate the Internet and technologies to advance their businesses. It's one of just a handful of technology-oriented magazines to survive the dot-com implosion. While many competitors confused readers with obscure dot-com marketing lingo, *Business 2.0* stuck to the basics, offering business people clear explanations of how technology works and how they can use it. Good stuff!

Like Shooting a Hole-In-One

Since I'm having so much fun with this, here's another example. Pixim is located in Mountain View, California. According to its website, the company "has developed an imaging platform that produces substantially higher-quality moving and still images than those available through any other existing technology. Called the Digital Pixel System platform or DPS, Pixim's imaging system delivers unmatched flexibility and functionality by combining image capture and processing within a single system."

The explanation sounds good. Exactly what Pixim does is still unclear to me, but it sounds impressive. Only after reading an article in *USA Today* did I learn that Pixim makes semiconductors, or chips, that power next-generation surveillance cameras. In addition, the technology can be used to help digital cameras adjust to bad lighting. In other words, Pixim will let you take better pictures. Oh, one more fact—Francis Ford Coppola is interested in Pixim's technology for advanced movie cameras.

I had to stop for a moment. Francis Ford Coppola is using the company's technology? There's the Wow! Funny, I didn't find that on the company's website. Why would you bury that piece of information? That's like shooting a hole-in-one on the seventeenth at Pebble Beach and not telling anyone about it. You'll get a "wow" out of any golfer for that accomplishment. You'll get a yawn from my wife, but then again, she wouldn't be the target audience for that particular message! You've got to know your audience.

In her book, *Use What You've Got,* New York real estate mogul Barbara Corcoran advises businesspeople to talk short and talk plain when a reporter calls. "You might feel more astute explaining to a reporter that 'market place conditions have declined somewhat and I have every confidence that the economic conditions will improve blah, blah, blah.' But if your competitor says, 'The market dumped,' that's the quote you'll see in the morning paper."

Lose the Jargon or Lose Your Audience

Great business communicators avoid mind-numbing jargon, especially when delivering to outsiders the message behind their service, product, company, or cause. As the president of a news and information company,

Devin Wenig describes the value of a message that's free from obscure acronyms, terms and words.

"I think in the post-nineties world, there is even more of a penalty to management jargon," Wenig says.

> I think people hide behind management jargon when they either don't understand the substance or they're not passionate about it. They use words and themes that a normal person walking down the street just wouldn't understand. People used a lot of jargon in the late '90s and it resulted with a bad taste in everyone's mouth. A presentation at an IPO road show that nobody could understand would result in a stock that shot up 900 percent. But there was no "there" there. It's not an option anymore to take your language down to a very simple, clear, and understandable level. I remove any words that I think I would have to explain—they come out.

Speaking without Saying Anything Isn't Anything at All!

Wenig makes a great point. In the late '90s, executives who infused their language with jargon that nobody could understand were rewarded by soaring stock prices or piles of cash. Not anymore. If you fancy yourself a '90s kind of presenter, you'll lose out to communicators who connect with contemporary audiences by talking plainly.

But I was still curious about something. I asked Wenig, "What happens when you're talking to a group that not only understands some of your company's jargon but expects you to use it?"

"There's nothing wrong with that," said Wenig.

> But that's different than using obscure words to hide concepts. So I might say "five thousand units of RET (Reuters Electronic Trading)." That's not hiding anything. Investor groups know what that is and there's nothing wrong in using that term. But I wouldn't say, "the positive trend that we noted in the first quarter continues in the second quarter, however that is offset by several different factors." Carmine, that's speaking without saying anything!

While I was writing this chapter, an Associated Press reporter, David McHugh, contributed an article from CeBIT, a giant technology trade show held in Europe once a year. The article, "Simplicity In, Jargon Out at Tech Fair," called attention to the trend of tech companies to "muffle the jargon" while clearly explaining the benefits of the technology to average consumers. "Simplicity" was in, McHugh wrote, while acronyms were out as marketing tools. That's what great contemporary communicators strive to do as well—explain concepts simply to touch the hearts and minds of their audiences. Jargon gets in the way.

★ ★ ★

Intuit founder, Scott Cook, on the appropriate use of jargon: "Carmine, jargon isn't inherently bad if it's what the customer uses to talk about their life, their products. We try to root our communication in the customer's words and experience. For example, if you're talking to investors, EPS (earnings per share) is jargon they really want to hear about. They want to know how you're going to grow earnings. Jargon isn't bad if it's the customer-preferred jargon."

The Fear That Leads to Jargon

Suze Orman said something interesting about jargon during my conversation with her. "How do you make complicated financial topics easy to understand?" I asked.

Orman said, "Too many people want to impress others with the information they have so others think the speaker is intelligent. I don't care what people think about it. All I care about is that the information I'm imparting empowers the listener or reader of my material. So I'm clear on the intention of why I'm delivering the information."

"But Suze," I said, "If you're message is too simple, don't you risk not being taken seriously? Even among some of my clients, they feel if they simplify the message too much, they risk losing credibility. How do you balance the two?"

"I disagree with your clients," Orman said.

Here's the key. You must not be afraid of criticism. If your intention is to impart a message that will create change for the person listening, then if you ask me, it is respectful to that person to make the message as simple as possible. For example, if I gave you directions to how to get to my house, you would want me to give you the simplest directions to get there. If I made it more complicated, you would not be better off. You might get aggravated and give up. If it were simple, chances are you will get in your car and try to get to my house rather than giving up and saying it's not worth it. Others criticize simplicity because they need to feel that it's more complicated. If everything were so simple, they think their jobs could be eliminated. It's our fear of extinction, our fear of elimination, our fear of not being important that leads us to communicate things in a more complex way than we need to.

USA Today's Secret Weapon

USA Today is America's most popular newspaper. Its appeal is simple— the stories are colorful, short, and easy to comprehend (usually without turning the page!). *USA Today* reporters take complicated subjects and turn them into easily digestible nuggets of information. Great business communicators do the same. Business presenters could learn a lot from *USA Today*.

Since 1985, Kevin Maney has been the leading technology columnist for *USA Today*. Most newspaper reporters would rather do what they do than talk about what they do, but Maney made an exception for this book. I'm glad he did. His insights are extraordinarily helpful for anyone looking to make their message more powerful, interesting, and simple!

During one of our conversations, I asked Maney how he makes extraordinarily complicated technologies so easy to understand. For starters, Maney considers jargon such a turn-off, he discards ninety-nine out of one hundred press releases he gets everyday. That means only one out of one hundred stories pitched by PR professionals succeeds in grabbing his attention. No wonder spokespeople who eliminate jargon stand out.

Maney says the majority of corporate pitches fail to get noticed because they are loaded with "politics"—too many people involved in crafting the corporate message.

Press releases get circulated around a company, often to every officer plus people directly involved. It's classic "too many cooks." Everyone has something they want to take out, put in, or change. And then legal gets hold of it and waters down the language or whatever it is they do to cover their butts. What's really happening here is that the press releases are being written for the wrong audience—for company executives, lawyers, and regulators—instead of for the press or the general public.

The problem Maney confronts applies to press releases and presentations. Remember that most speaking presentations begin with some form of material that's been written down and, in many cases, approved by superiors. The same problems that result in bad press releases can ruin presentations.

Making Sense of the Invisible

Maney's writing is effective because he uses clear, direct, and simple language. Take the nanotechnology industry for instance. Few companies are as complex as those in this field. Simply put, nanotech is manipulating atoms to create new products. Trouble is, few nanotech scientists can explain what they do in simple terms. If you ever attend a nanotech conference, bring Motrin. Your brain will hurt. Guaranteed. Maney does an amazing job of doing what nanotech executives should be doing, explaining the implications of their work in clear, simple language free of jargon.

Here's one example. A company called Nanosys describes itself on its website like this:

> Nanosys is an industry leading nanotechnology company developing nano-enabled systems based on a platform technology incorporating patent-protected, high performance, and highly integrated inorganic semiconductor nanostructures.

Sounds simple, doesn't it? I asked Maney, who has written about the company, how he would describe the firm in a way my grandmother could understand. Maney said he starts by using accessible words, calling Nanosys a company "messing" with atoms to do things never before possible. "Carmine, the problem with corporate PR is that nobody is willing to use the words like messing." Accessible words, Maney argues, are critical to explaining complex topics. Maney also uses easy-to-grasp examples.

So here's what we have: Nanosys, according to Maney, is a company messing with atoms to make new coatings like super-water-resistant material. The result could be windshields that don't need wipers or clothes that could be worn in water and remain dry. Now isn't that a lot easier to understand and more interesting than the company's own description? Of course it is. Leave it to a *USA Today* journalist to make sense of it for us. That's the problem. Maney shouldn't have to work at it. Neither should your customers, investors, or outsiders. By the way, please don't think your message is more complicated than the manipulation of molecules at the atomic level. It's not.

★ ★ ★

Quick nanotech story—I remember my first meeting with a group of executives to help revitalize a trade show called Wescon. It had once been one of the largest engineering shows in the country, but had seen its attendance steadily decline as it struggled to remain relevant and competitive. The organizers had a good idea to co-locate a nanotech conference along with the traditional show. I saw the potential in leveraging the nanotech angle to raise the conference's visibility among the media, exhibitors, and attendees.

Our messaging campaign, with a heavy focus on nanotech, was highly successful. But it started out shaky when I asked scientists involved in the conference to explain the importance of nanotech to the engineers who might attend. I was completely lost, as were most of the others watching the presentation. The next day I bought a book intended to explain the technology to the average reader. *The Next Big Thing Is Really Small* was short (under two hundred pages) and literally kept me turning every page. The first few sentences could not have been more compelling: "Imagine materials one hundred times stronger than steel but one-sixth the weight. Cheap, supersonic transportation. Computers millions of times more powerful and efficient than those that exist today. The development of a host of cancer-curing drugs…you might be tempted to dismiss such predictions as unlikely or impossible. Don't."

I went back to the Wescon project invigorated and ready to spread the gospel of nanotech. Our press release, titled "Wescon: Inventing the Future One Atom at a Time," was a hit. Attendance rose, the sales staff sold more booth space, newspapers covered it, and the former mayor of San Francisco, Willie Brown, even paid a well-publicized visit to the convention. Simplicity and clarity saved the day!

The Perfect Wardrobe Isn't Perfect without the Right Accessories

It's not enough to tell a story as we discussed in "Simple Secret #2: Inspiration." You've got to tell a great story to stand out. Just like the perfect suit, the perfect accessories make the look complete. Top spokespeople dress up their stories with: analogies, anecdotes, endorsements, examples, statistics, and testimonials. Let's look at some examples.

Story Enhancer	Sample
Analogy	"The ratcheting up of compensation has been obscene. There is a tendency to put cocker spaniels on compensation committees, not Doberman pinschers."—*Warren Buffett*
Anecdote	"Dow Jones credited us with helping them publish the *Wall Street Journal* the day after 9/11. Let me describe what happened to the paper that day and how we mobilized our team to fix the problem." —*Gallo Communications Group Client, Expert Server Group*
Endorsement	"For its annual 'Top 100' list of best products, CNET chose the HP Photosmart 7550 for the 'Best Affordable Photo Printer' and the HP LaserJet 2300 for the 'Best Small-Business Workgroup Laser.'" —*Hewlett Packard*

Story Enhancer	Sample
Example	"As systems supplier for many companies... we're also in a lot of places that you may not realize. Because we supply servers to Sony and power Nike's supply chain, we're there when you hit your alarm clock in the morning and put on your running shoes."—*Carly Fiorina, Former CEO, Hewlett Packard*
Statistic	"We sold 336,000 iPods in one quarter. That is two and a half iPods sold every minute, twenty-four hours a day, seven days a week last quarter."—*Steve Jobs*
Testimonial	"At Starbucks, we're proud to be among *Fortune*'s 100 Best Places to Work." —*Starbucks*

Fortune magazine tackled the issue of executive charisma in a January, 1996 article: "Charismatic people have a remarkable ability to distill complex ideas into simple messages. What's their secret? They communicate by using symbols, analogies, metaphors, and stories. If they're really charismatic, the guys on the factory floor, even the janitors, understand their pitch." You, too, can reach the point when everyone understands your pitch by adopting some of the tools in the table.

Here again we can learn a lot from *USA Today*'s Kevin Maney who uses analogies to make complicated technologies easy to understand. I asked Maney for one of his favorite examples of turning a complex technology into plain English. He referred to an article he wrote about a company called VMware. According to the company's site, it "builds innovative and useful software products that leverage our state-of-the-art technology in several areas, most notably in the virtualization of the x86 architecture and in full hardware resource management." It's a good bet that Jack Welch would have a serious problem with that explanation.

The explanation was too complicated for Maney. He came up with a brilliant analogy. According to Maney, "I was looking for a way to explain something that was almost inexplicable in a way that my kids could get. I have no idea how I thought of cooking and pots as a way to explain server virtualization, but I put it this way: Say you're cooking. You have four pots on four burners. In them are a stew, mashed potatoes, corn, and peas. One pot per dish. If you could virtualize your pots the way VMware virtualizes a computer, you'd have a lot more flexibility. If one burner went out, you could put the peas in with the mashed potatoes, but the peas would cook just as if they were still in the pea pot, and the mashed potatoes would cook as if they were alone in the mashed potato pot. You might discover that you have a lot of extra room in each pot, and that you could cook two or three dishes in a single virtual pot, then shut down a couple of burners to save costs."

Maney thought VM's engineers would hate what he wrote. Far from it. They thought it was great, and it gave them a way of explaining their own company in pitches and presentations. This is Maney at his best, using simple analogies to take the complexity out of complicated subjects. But again, it's not Maney's job to make sense out of your service, product, company, or cause. It's your responsibility as a spokesperson.

★ ★ ★

While covering the Schwarzenegger administration, I watched countless presentations from the governor as he tried to convince voters across the state to back two measures on the March 2, 2004 ballot—Propositions 57 and 58. The first proposition was a $15 billion dollar bond to help pay off California's massive debt, the second proposition would put a spending cap on future spending. Both propositions had to pass for either to go into effect. I was amazed at the number of skeptical individuals who changed their minds by the end of Schwarzenegger's fifteen-minute presentation. It was also the first time I ever saw a governor use PowerPoint.

Schwarzenegger used a simple analogy that everyone could grasp. "It's like this," he would say. "If you had maxed out several credit cards, a financial counselor would recommend that you consolidate that debt into one low interest loan then cut up your cards. That's what propositions 57 and 58 intend to do."

After one presentation, a member of the audience said to me, "Cutting up credit cards. I like that idea." Schwarzenegger's explanation was clear. It was also consistent. In a five-week period before the election, I counted more than sixty newspaper articles quoting Schwarzenegger's credit-card analogy. But one week before the election, polls showed the measures trailing among voters. I spoke to one Republican lawmaker who was sure it would be defeated. I wasn't so sure, especially after seeing how listeners changed their mind after the presentations. Schwarzenegger, as always, remained optimistic. "Failure is not an option," he would say.

On the day of the election, Propositions 57 and 58 passed overwhelmingly. A victory so convincing that it gave Schwarzenegger power to convince the legislature to get to work implementing the rest of his vision for California.

The Salesman Behind Salesforce

Before Marc Benioff founded Salesforce.com, he thrived in sales at Oracle. According to an article in the *San Francisco Chronicle* on September 3, 2002, "Benioff, as a little-known manager, made a presentation to thousands of Oracle senior salespeople that had them jumping around and singing as if they were at a revival meeting....An iconoclast with a grand vision, the San Francisco resident can sell almost anyone he meets on the Salesforce.com way of thinking." With an ability like that, it's no wonder that Benioff went on to become the top salesman at Oracle and to create his own successful software company that has captured the imagination of the industry, not to mention the concern of his competitors.

I had already been impressed with Benioff's communication skills before the company hired me to work with some of its top executives. Benioff follows the advice in this chapter to the letter: He finds the Wow, keeps his message free from jargon, and uses story enhancers.

In just one interview for the June 2003 issue of *Selling Power* magazine, Benioff makes liberal use of analogies, examples, stories, and statistics to make his case and dispel his critics. He tells the story of how he originally came up with the idea behind Salesforce.com: "It was the beginning of the Internet, and I was using this incredible application called Amazon.com...And I said, 'Why can't all enterprise software be exactly like this?'"

Benioff uses analogies to describe his radical vision of delivering software via a pipeline, like water or electricity, paying for it as you go: "Take water," he says. "You don't pay for water five years in advance...the same for sanitation and electricity...so why is it with enterprise software that we're making people pay for septic services years in advance? It makes no sense when there's a modern network."

Benioff even uses an analogy to explain his relationship with his former boss, now his competitor: "I compare business to tennis," Benioff says. "Larry Ellison, Tom Siebel, Craig Conway of Peoplesoft—all competitors of mine, and I'm playing tennis. I hit the ball over the net, the ball comes back, and it goes back and forth. But when we walk off the court we should still be friends."

★ ★ ★

As CEO of advertising giant Young and Rubicam, Ann Fudge is one of the highest-ranking African American women in the corporate world. She's mastered the 10 Simple Secrets including the ability to craft a message so direct, so simple, and so compelling that she wins over a variety of audiences. "She is equally comfortable with consumers at the ballpark, factory workers on a production line, and executives in a boardroom," says one former boss.

Can you sell anyone on your way of thinking? Imagine what you could accomplish if you could: raise your visibility, inspire your employees, attract investors, and make more sales. The world's greatest business communicators have this ability because they've mastered the fifth Simple Secret. They keep their messages simple and clear. A simple message is easier to remember. And a message that's easier to remember is easier to act upon.

Now that it's clear to you that clarity is key, it's time to reveal the sixth Simple Secret of all great business communicators.

1. **Take the *USA Today* Test.** Ask yourself, how would *USA Today* describe my service, product, company, or cause? Start reading it. Pay attention to the headlines and the first paragraph of the story. How does it hook you? Read the columns by Kevin Maney and the other excellent writers. They're experts at making subjects clear, simple, and concise.

2. **Use the Internet.** There are several resources on the Internet that will help you cut the jargon from your corporate messaging.

A. Bullfighter: Deloitte Consulting has developed a software program to help you identify jargon in your documents. It's called Bullfighter, guaranteed to "strip the bull out of business." You can find it at www.dc.com/bullfighter. Try it to see just how much jargon you might have in your own material. It's a free software download that runs in your Microsoft Word or PowerPoint programs. As the developers say, "Unless you believe in expressions like 'value-based paradigm shift' or in multisyllabic sentences that run on for ages, you owe it to your loved ones and coworkers to try it." Hey, it's free. You don't have anything to lose except your jargon.

B. Plain English: A friend of mine, Kevin Ryan, author of *Write Up the Corporate Ladder,* introduced me to a UK-based Plain English Campaign (www.plainenglish.co.uk). According to the site, it's an independent pressure group fighting for public information to be written in plain English. It has plenty of before-and-after examples that would be hilarious if they weren't true! Here's my favorite:
Before
If there are any points on which you require explanation or further particulars we shall be glad to furnish such additional details as may be required by telephone.
After
If you have any questions, please ring.

C. Buzzkiller: Visit this site at www.buzzkiller.net. The organizers behind this web resource are dedicated to purging the language of empty, senseless, and overused marketing terms. I've caught myself using some of these words on more than one occasion!

Utter bilge frequently related to technology	General-interest business drivel
• solution(s) • robust • turnkey • interactive • best of breed • mission-critical • scalable • next-generation • Web-enabled • B2B, B2C • e-tailing • seamless • end-to-end • "the ___ space" • offline • incent (vt) • end user • architecting • deliverables *Source: Buzzkiller.Net*	• leading • synergy • leverage (vt) • core competencies • best practices • bottom line • 24/7 • out of the loop • on the ground • benchmark • value-added • proactive • win-win • think outside the box • fast track • result-driven • empower • knowledge base • at the end of the day

SIMPLE SECRET #6: BREVITY
KEEP IT SHORT. PERIOD.

"The ultimate success factor for anybody in a leadership position is the ability to communicate with passion, clarity, and conciseness."

SYBASE CEO JOHN CHEN

"Communication is responsible for 90 percent of my success, without a doubt."

NEW YORK REAL ESTATE QUEEN
BARBARA CORCORAN

John F. Kennedy galvanized the nation in 1961 with an inaugural address scripted for fifteen minutes. Think about it. In fifteen minutes, Kennedy shared a vision that inspired generations, changed social policies in the '60s, and helped to land a man on the moon by the end of the decade. The world's greatest communicators, in business or politics, keep it brief. If I'd have it my way, this chapter would end here. Since my publisher might take exception, I'll keep 'em happy by expanding on the topic. But not by much!

The most persuasive speakers are their own best editors. They cut, cut, and cut some more. In his magnificent book about the Kennedy years, *A Thousand Days,* Arthur Schlesinger said Kennedy was an excellent editor, "skilled at tuning up thoughts and eliminating verbal excess." In *Kennedy,* JFK's primary speechwriter Ted Sorensen wrote that Kennedy would use one syllable words instead of three syllables when appropriate, or one word instead of two or three words to say the same thing. Ah, now it makes sense that Kennedy would use "foes" instead of "adversaries." Kennedy kept his speeches—his presentations—as tight as possible. Actually, it was George Washington who set the tone for brevity. His second inaugural address was only 135 words!

Now ask yourself, do I really need sixty minutes and fifty-two PowerPoint slides to tell the story behind my service, product, company, or cause? Can I cut something out? I'll bet you can and your presentation will be stronger for it. (I'm not exaggerating about the fifty-two PowerPoint slides. A client of mine once had fifty-two PowerPoint slides he planned to show in a one-hour presentation. My gosh, I thought, after this presentation lawmakers are going to have to come up with a new crime category—death by PowerPoint. We reduced the presentation to thirty slides. Still too many for me, but some people are as reluctant to eliminate a slide as they would be to give up their own child. I've learned to pick my battles.)

The editors of a weekly business journal in Silicon Valley once asked me to contribute columns on the topic of business communications. My first article came in at fourteen hundred words. I felt pretty pleased with myself until the editor told me it would have to be cut in half to no more than seven hundred words! I got over it. That's the life of a journalist. It can always be shorter. But in this case, I really thought the story needed room to "breathe." (That's the term I use when I don't want editors to cut down my copy. They seem to prefer the term "wordy.") But I had no choice. Cut the column in half or it doesn't run. The final column was 694 words. The editors loved it, as did the magazine's readers. Truth be told, it was much more interesting than my initial draft because it forced me to get to the point.

San Jose Mercury technology writer Mike Langberg once described the scene of a show called Demo that's held annually in Scottsdale, Arizona. It's a chance for companies to introduce their products to hundreds of influential listeners including venture capitalists, buyers, analysts, and journalists. Langberg wrote, "A successful performance at Demo gets your company publicity, customers, funding, and maybe even a buyout offer." Out of two hundred fifty companies that hope to present, only seventy are chosen. But in order to win, presentations are limited to six minutes. Some are held to just sixty seconds! How would you perform if you had one minute to pitch your product? One company successfully generated excitement in that short a time—Palm—launching the first Palm Pilot at Demo in 1996.

People Buy from People

John Chen is CEO of Sybase, a $2 billion business software firm. Chen grew up poor in Hong Kong. He would read *The Adventures of Tom Sawyer* and dream of the adventures he, too, might find in America. Not only did Chen find adventure, but wealth, success, and power. From Hong Kong, he made his way to a New England high school and later attended Brown University to major in engineering. In 1979, he received a Master's from the California Institute of Technology. After a string of successes over the following years, Chen joined Sybase in 1997 and became its chairman and CEO a year later.

According to the *Contra Costa Times,* "His [Chen's] new job was one of the least enviable in the software industry…Beaten down by a series of missteps and three straight years of losses, cash-strapped Sybase seemed on the verge of imploding…Chen saw what others didn't: good technology, loyal customers, a solid brand name."

Fast forward to April 2004 Sybase reports a net income of $84 million for 2003 after a net loss of $94.7 million the year before. It's a strong leader in the mobile and wireless space (Sybase software allows a salesperson in the field to be immediately notified of a price increase by cell phone or personal digital assistant). Its stock, once at $4.50, trades at $22. Its value skyrockets. Writers credit Chen for his vision, fiscal prudence, and for keeping employees and customers motivated during the downturn. He even joins Disney's board of directors. Not bad for someone who grew up poor in China and could hardly carry a conversation when he first arrived in America.

I had the pleasure of interviewing Chen several times on television. When it came time to write this book, despite his very heavy travel schedule, Chen generously offered to reveal the secrets behind his success as a business communicator. And speak he does. Not a week goes by that he doesn't give at least two or three presentations. One typical week goes like this: a speech for one thousand senior executives in Japan; several smaller forums for employees, customers, and prospects; a keynote for a leadership conference in Shanghai, China; a dinner speech for the mayor of Shanghai; followed by presentations to employees and radio/TV interviews in Hong Kong. All in one week!

"Why do you maintain such a heavy speaking schedule?" I asked Chen.

"People buy from people," Chen said.

And they want to buy from leaders who they can relate to. This is a very important part of my job, even more so with the investment community. They will not invest in your stock if they don't get a good feel for you as a person. They are looking for believability, integrity, honesty, and commitment. If I just recite what you can find on my website, it will be a complete failure. They will probably sell the stock because they'll say this guy doesn't have any passion (Secret #1), any commitment. He'll be wearing another badge tomorrow saying the same thing! They need to feel that you're excited about the future (Secret #2). It's only then that they go to the numbers to see if they back up what you're saying. Big investors like Fidelity, Oppenheimer, and Salomon do not invest in a company without thoroughly knowing the CEO and CFO—are these guys honest? Are these guys for real? Or is it just a bunch of PowerPoints? Customers and employees feel the same way. I do a lot of webcasts because employees like information and communication. It does more for morale when you have Q&A. If you come across as experienced, confident, substantive, employees feel good! If you're shifty and assign blame, employees feel you don't know what you're talking about or how you're going to get it done.

"Okay, John," I continued. "You explained why communication is such an important part of your job, but why do you try to keep presentations short?"

"You will lose the audiences' focus if you overdose on information," Chen said.

The bigger the audience, the more concise you must be. People have short attention spans. The audience will tune out if you keep going. If you can't grab them in the first ten words, you probably won't hold their attention long and people will be afraid to ask questions because they don't want to hear you ramble!

★ ★ ★

"I think Alan 'Ace' Greenberg, the former chairman of Bear Stearns, is a fantastic corporate speaker. He is straight to the point, willing to have some fun, and doesn't let anyone talk too long or pontificate about irrelevant subjects. He always moves speeches and meetings along at a record pace. He is famous in New York for hosting charity benefit dinners that never drag on and allows the audience to get home by 9:30 p.m."

David Moore, venture capitalist and Broadway comic

Her Friends Call Her Condi

Great business communicators speak in short, powerful sound bites, no matter how complex the issue. Brevity is powerful and persuasive. In September 2002, the Bush administration was preparing the public for an attack on Iraq to oust Saddam Hussein. As you might recall, the plan (and subsequent attack) sparked widespread protests not only in the U.S. but around the world. Regardless of your position on war or its outcome, there's no question the administration did an effective job of persuading the American public to support it (support began to erode as the original premise for attacking Iraq—finding weapons of mass destruction—came into question). United States secretary of state Condoleezza Rice demonstrated her mastery of the 10 Simple Secrets as she made the round of talk shows to argue the case for war. Rice is a great speaker, explaining complex topics in simple terms everyone can understand. She exudes class—in dress and in speech. Rice defends controversial decisions with confidence, clarity, and conciseness. When CNN's Wolf Blitzer questioned Rice, then national security advisor, about a possible attack on September 8, 2002, he got right to the point as did she.

Blitzer: Is Iraq's regime of President Saddam Hussein right now a clear and present danger to the United States?

Rice: There is no doubt that Saddam Hussein's regime is a danger to the United States and to its allies and to our interests. It is also a danger that is gathering momentum, and it simply makes no sense to wait any longer to do something about the threat that is posed here. As the president has said, "The one option that we do not have is to do nothing."

That's it. Yes, Hussein is a danger. He's getting worse. We have no other option. Regardless of your position, I think you'll agree that Rice's answers are short, powerful, and to the point. Dr. Rice's answers in the rest of the interview were equally as direct, equally as succinct. There's power in being concise. "Condi" knows it. You can achieve this power as well. Be brief. Be concise.

The Six-Second Sound Bite

The public's desire for brevity is universal. Nobody wants to hear you ramble, whether it's an audience in America, Asia, or Europe. Why? This time, you really can blame it on the media. The media has changed everything. Most people who have read newspapers, watched television news or entertainment programs, or listened to radio talk shows over the past decade have become accustomed to more content crammed into less space or time. When I hosted a radio show in San Francisco, I was advised to limit callers to no more than two minutes to keep it moving. Ever wonder why Sean Hannity, Dr. Laura, or Larry King keep the pressure on their callers? National Public Radio may be an exception, but who do you think gets the higher ratings? On radio and television, shorter is better. Today CNN brings you everything that happened in the world of entertainment in the "Hollywood Minute," Fox goes one better bringing us "The World in Eighty Seconds."

We've become sound bite addicts. A sound bite is a journalism term for a brief statement taken from a longer audio or videotaped news report. As best-selling author Harry Beckwith puts it, "the sound bite has replaced the paragraph as a unit of thought." Well, if the sound bite is the unit of thought, why do most spokespeople talk like they're presenting a Master's thesis?

When I took my first broadcast journalism course at Northwestern's Medill School of Journalism, we were taught to keep sound bites to no more than twenty seconds. Twenty seconds seems like an eternity today where six seconds is more common. Try it yourself. Use a stopwatch next time a news story cuts to a snippet from an interview. Be quick or you'll miss it. The length of television stories is getting shorter as well. When I went to graduate school, a two-minute "package" was acceptable. Today, you'd only get that amount of time if you had discovered Jimmy Hoffa. A Los Angeles station once wanted me to kick off the news show with a story no longer than one minute and five seconds. We're also faced with faster edits with half-second frames of video—thank you MTV and *Entertainment Tonight*!

★ ★ ★

"Today we are all tuned to receive information much more quickly, and we get bored in a hurry if things slow down. The video age has sped up our cognitive powers. We get to the point faster."
Fox News chairman Roger Ailes in *You Are the Message*

Whether you like it or not, we now live in a sound-bite society. Let's save the discussion on the pros and cons of this trend for the Harvard Debate Society. It's a fact and frankly, it doesn't bother me. There are plenty of outlets that cater to readers or listeners who want more discussion.

Successful presenters go for ratings. They don't bemoan the fact that audiences want them to keep their presentations short. They accept it. So should you. Great communicators not only recognize that audiences expect brevity, they use it to their advantage. They keep everything short—they give fifteen-second answers to questions and keep their presentations or speeches to no more than twenty minutes. I know what you're thinking: "But Carmine, I need much more time to describe the amazing benefits my customers are going to receive from using our products." Keep telling yourself that as competitors pass you by with a pitch that's more dynamic, simpler, and shorter.

Long is dull. Are you dull? I wouldn't know, but this much I can say—few of your colleagues, customers, or supervisors will tell you. As a communications coach, I often hear what you don't. One especially colorful CEO hired me to work with his sales executives. Once he closed the door to his office, he told me that one man "exuded the confidence of a beaten dog." Another sales manager was "shy, stiff, and weak." The third talks like a "slow drip…you want to tear your hair out waiting for him to get to the point." This particular sales team was actually doing quite well (you wouldn't know it by listening to their boss), but I understood what he was trying to say. They droned on and on when they would have had more impact by keeping it short. They all lacked pizzazz!

The Window of Impact

DILBERT reprinted by permission of United Feature Syndicate, Inc.

Obviously, your next staff meeting, speech, or presentation will last longer than six seconds. But you get the point; shorter is better. When it comes to presentations, fifteen to twenty minutes is what I call the "Window of Impact" to get your message across. Studies have shown that our attention span isn't that long. Audience retention drops off dramatically after approximately eighteen minutes. The segments on the television show *60 Minutes* run no longer than fifteen to seventeen minutes. The Great Communicator himself, Ronald Reagan, gave strict instructions to his speechwriters to avoid writing speeches that lasted longer than twenty minutes. Not because he wanted to go back to the White House for a nap, but because his training as an actor and public speaker taught him what government researchers and *60 Minutes* producers already knew—shorter is better.

Studies have shown that listeners retain up to 90 percent of what they hear in a twenty-minute block of time. As the length of a presentation gets longer, listeners remember less and less. Even if your particular presentation takes a half-day's worth of activities, keep the Window of Impact in mind—vary the presentation materials every twenty minutes.

★ ★ ★

Most companies will spend an eternity creating the mission statement, a defining purpose. Mission statements should be clear and concise, exactly what most are not. I asked *Dilbert* creator Scott Adams what he thought of mission statements. Adams said "a mission statement is a long awkward sentence that demonstrates management's inability to think clearly."

"Why do you think so many executives have trouble getting to the point?" I asked Adams.

Adams gave the classic *Dilbert* response: "The person who talks the longest seems to be the most knowledgeable no matter what they said. Clearly, they're indispensable."

Keep It Short or Be Shown the Door

As executive director for venture capital giant 3i, Martin Gagen helped direct the company's investments in more than two thousand companies across Europe, the U.S., and Asia. 3i originally hired me to work with some of its managing directors to help prepare them for their media interviews. I came to know Gagen and grew fond of his communication style. He knows what works and what doesn't.

During one of our interviews for this book, I asked Gagen, "How many presentations have you seen?"

"Thousands," he said. "I've been in the venture capital business for twenty-five years. I see ten presentations a week."

"And how would you describe most of them?" I asked.

"The majority are boring," he said. "The biggest defect is that they never cut to the chase quickly. The bad ones are the ones that go on and after an hour you have to interrupt and ask, what is it that you are really trying to say?"

"How much time would it take me, as an entrepreneur, to grab your attention?" I asked.

> I will know in the first five to ten minutes. You've either got my attention or you've lost it. That's why you need to tell me what the point of your company is off the bat. If you only have five minutes, what would you say? If you then have twenty minutes, you can support the main points, but it's still five minutes of key material. In fact, if you're given twenty minutes, take fifteen. The meeting can go longer because of questions. But fifteen minutes should be all it takes to tell me what you're going to tell me. You've already got the audience. Don't confuse meeting length with attention-grabbing length. They are completely different things.

Venture capitalists, with millions of dollars at stake, understand the Window of Impact. Can a bad presentation about a truly groundbreaking technology still attract funding? Sure it can. But according to Gagen, a bad spokesperson makes it harder for listeners to grasp the company's true potential.

> We're human beings first, business people second. You react emotionally to people. I am happy to back a business where the leader is a little dull but he absolutely knows his stuff and he's doing all the right things and business is great. I'm just going to have to work harder to get there because my first impression is holy smoke, I can't put him in front of an investor syndicate, I can't put him on stage to promote his company, I can't put him on a road show. Those are issues to overcome.

I believe those issues can be overcome. But you must first recognize the fact that longer isn't always better, especially when it comes to the art of persuasion.

When asked to give a speech or presentation, venture capitalist Martin Gagen divides his talk into four themes. "If you've done a good job preparing your message," says Gagen, "then ninety-nine times out of one hundred, you'll only have four things to say. Brevity involves how much packaging you'll include around four points." For example, when discussing the venture capital business, Gagen sticks with four themes: The recent trends in global economics; a discussion of capital; where venture capital fits in; and what the future might hold. According to Gagen, "In each theme I drop a couple of facts because the audience loves having learned something they didn't know. You've got to balance the fifty-thousand-foot statement and details." Gagen achieves that balance by sticking to just four key themes but giving his audience some facts they can use at their next dinner party.

The Short Story of NYC's Broker to the Stars

Barbara Corcoran is a motivational dynamo, a great speaker, and very, very wealthy. She started New York's premier real estate firm, The Corcoran Group, with a $1,000 loan from a boyfriend. The relationship fizzled but the loan grew. Twenty-five years later, The Corcoran Group accounts for $5 billion in sales and is considered among New York's premier real estate firms, thanks in large part to Corcoran's ability to touch the hearts and minds of her clients. Corcoran has since sold the Corcoran Group to NRT for a reported $70 million dollars. Not a bad return for a $1,000 loan.

Corcoran spent a lot of time with me as we tried to identify the secrets behind her success as a communicator. Like most of the personalities interviewed for this book, I can talk about her in any chapter, but she has some very insightful things to say on this topic. For instance, in any communication, whether it's on the phone or behind a podium, Corcoran believes in cutting to the chase.

"People are not as interested in you as you think they are," Corcoran said.

Once the spotlight is on you, you begin to think that you are the most important person in the room and everything you have to say is soooo very important. And it's just not true. I think you have to be hyper-paranoid about how succinct you are and respect the listener's time…Important people think they're very busy. But the fact of the matter is everyone is very busy. They simply don't have the time to hear the details—unless it's a story, but even then you need to get rid of the excess.

Corcoran's conversations last no longer than they have to. She especially likes to keep her speeches short. If she's scheduled to speak for thirty or forty minutes, Corcoran will speak for all of twelve minutes and spend the rest of the time answering questions. She says it's her way of communicating in a "rushed world." I say it's her standard for meeting the requirements for the Window of Impact. Corcoran gets it. It works for her. Corcoran is known as a motivational speaker. But part of her appeal is her ability to hit her key themes fast.

Brevity Is the Soul of Wisdom

My friend Kevin Ryan wrote a terrific book about business writing called *Write Up the Corporate Ladder*.

"Why should business communicators keep their messages short?" I asked Ryan.

"For stand-up comics, brevity is the soul of wit," he said.

For business communicators brevity is the soul of wisdom. When comics break this golden rule, they flop. They get immediate negative audience feedback. Unfortunately, when businesspeople break this rule their audiences sit quietly and attentively, which gives the speakers a false sense of success. If every audience booed a businessperson who took up its valuable time with an hour-long presentation that could have been given in fifteen minutes, verbosity wouldn't be a problem in the business world today—and productivity across the board would probably increase 15 percent.

"But Kevin," I asked, "What if it's highly complex and substantive information? Should we expect executives to write or speak in sound bites?"

"Yes, as long as the sound bites are interesting, new, and fresh," he said. "People turn off clichés and 'the party line.' If the information is highly complex and substantive, it is the job of the speaker to present the essence of his or her complex ideas in a clear and concise statement that makes me want to learn more."

"It sounds like contemporary audiences are changing," I said. "Do you think the average attention span is getting shorter?"

"The culprits here," said Ryan, "are the constant bombardment of information—from billboards to cable TV and the Internet—plus the non-stop lifestyles most people lead, which leave them scant time to read or listen to any medium that doesn't directly affect their jobs or personal lives." Regardless of the culprits, as a speaker you've got to respect the needs of contemporary audiences. By doing so, you'll make a stronger impact.

Twenty-five Words or Less

As I was working on this chapter, I read a newspaper article about a "fast-pitch" competition in Southern California. Tech Coast Angels is one of the largest angel investor groups in the country, made up of wealthy individuals who fund promising start-up firms. The fast-pitch contest was meant to separate the potential winners from the deadly duds. Thirty-six firms were invited to participate; twelve would get to present in front of the entire group of five hundred investors. Here's the catch: they only had sixty seconds to make their case. I couldn't help but wonder how many small firms lost the opportunity to become big firms because their spokespeople failed to make a compelling case in sixty seconds. In any business, how many people fail to bring their companies or careers to the next level because they lack a lead? Far too many, I'm afraid. According to organizers of the fast pitch competition, only .017 of all business plans submitted to investors succeed in getting funded.

Here's an exercise—if you only had twenty-five words to describe your service, product, company, or cause, how would you do it? In June 2004, *Business 2.0* devoted an issue to profiling the one hundred fastest-growing tech companies. The magazine's editor, Josh Quittner, challenged his reporters to say in twenty-five words or less why a particular company should be included on the list. For example, why is San Diego's Qualcomm growing so fast? According to *Business 2.0,* because "Qualcomm technology powered forty-six million phones sold in Asia last year and will have Verizon Wireless customers surfing at broadband speeds by 2005." That's it. If someone asks the Qualcomm executives why their company would make a good investment, those twenty-three words would make the point better than most marketing material.

In *What Clients Love,* Harry Beckwith writes, "If you cannot describe what makes you different and excellent in twenty-five words or less, don't fix your copy. Fix your company." Agreed. Try it. It's a good exercise. Beckwith reminds us that Thomas Jefferson only chose twenty-two words as the inscription on his tombstone. The man who drafted the Declaration of Independence, served as the third president of the United States, and founded the University of Virginia only chose twenty-two words to describe his life's accomplishments:

Author of the Declaration of American Independence
of the Statute of Virginia for Religious Freedom
and Father of the University of Virginia.

I hope this chapter has helped you appreciate the power of conciseness. Respect your listener's time by eliminating excessive words in presentations, meetings, speeches, or interviews. In turn, they will respect you and your message. You'll stand a better chance of being heard.

Now that you've learned the secrets to grabbing and keeping the attention of your listeners, it's time to reveal the last three Simple Secrets that will help you seal the deal.

★ COACHING DRILLS ★

1. **Identify Key Themes.** Venture capitalist Martin Gagen likes to keep his talks to no more than four themes with supporting facts, figures, and stories. See if you can keep your next presentations to four themes or less. Can you?

_____

_____

_____

_____

_____

2. *Write Up the Corporate Ladder.* In this excellent book by Kevin Ryan, you can learn how to succeed in the workplace by presenting your written ideas clearly and persuasively. Instead of relying on rules and mechanics, Ryan introduces a new, simplified approach to writing that emphasizes the importance of the "writer's intuition" and "message over mechanics." Good writing will help improve your overall presentations because most public speaking starts with a written word. Give it a read!

3. **Twenty-five Words or Less.** Remember how the editor of *Business 2.0* challenged his writers to describe a company in twenty-five words or less, or how Jefferson could describe the highlights of his extraordinary life in even fewer words (funny how he omits being President of the United States)? What would you omit if you only had twenty-five words to describe your service, product, company, or cause? What would you include? It's a good exercise. Try it!

_____

_____

_____

_____

_____

4. **PowerPoint Tip:** Keeping the words you use on your PowerPoint slides to a minimum will help you deliver your presentation more concisely.

How many words per slide? That's a good question. I've heard the "Rule of Three" (Three lines down and three words across), the "Rule of Five," etc. Frankly, I think a dynamic speaker can make the presentation come alive whether a slide has three lines or six. But after watching countless presentations and speaking to the world's top experts on PowerPoint presentations, I'd suggest you stick to the following advice: Since groups of three are easy to digest, try to stick to three lines down, three words across. However, don't be a stickler for rules. If the content warrants, feel comfortable with four by four (four lines down, four words across) but don't ever create a slide with more than six lines down and four words across. Well, you can. Nobody's stopping you. But you'll lose power as a speaker by using too many words when fewer will do.

PART THREE

BLOW 'EM AWAY BY TALKING,
WALKING, AND LOOKING
LIKE A LEADER

Now that you've successfully crafted and articulated a message your audience cares about, it's time to talk, walk, and look like a leader. The great business communicators you'll hear from in chapters 7 through 9 use their voice and body to capture the hearts, minds and souls of their listeners.

The captivating tools showcased in this section will teach you how to:

- Deliver your message with power and confidence
- Exude a commanding presence over everyone in the room
- Dress and look the part of a leader who people will invest in, buy from, and follow anywhere

Let's continue your transformation by improving the way you deliver the story you've crafted. It's time to reveal Simple Secret #7.

SIMPLE SECRET #7: SAY IT WITH STYLE

WHAT GREAT TELEVISION ANCHORS KNOW
THAT YOU DON'T

"My whole career has been writing for the ear, and this is how you do it: in relatively short sentences that impart information quickly."

PEGGY NOONAN

Justin Sullivan/Getty Images

"Larry [Ellison] is fantastic at creating excitement–over and over again."

AUTHOR STUART READ
WRITING ABOUT ORACLE'S CEO
IN *THE ORACLE EDGE*

On Saturday night, October 11, 2003, I spent three hours at a small Italian restaurant listening to the stories of a man whose feat will never be outdone; former astronaut Neil Armstrong. Think about it. A baseball player who hits seventy-three home runs in a single season like Giants left-fielder Barry Bonds expects that record to be broken someday. Bill Gates may be the wealthiest man in the world, but someday, somebody will be richer. But if you're the first man to step foot on the moon, nobody will ever break your record. First man to step foot on the moon—wouldn't that be a nice accomplishment to add to your resumé?

I joined Armstrong thanks to a family friend who set up dinner for a group of us. During dinner, after a few glasses of a fine Barolo, somebody in the group had the courage to ask Armstrong what all of us had been thinking: "Did you come up with, 'One Small Step for Man, One Giant Leap for Mankind,' or did someone at NASA tell you to say it?" For the record, the thought originated with Armstrong. During dinner, I kept thinking about those ten memorable words and how they were delivered, with just the right pause for dramatic effect: One Small Step for Man... One Giant Leap for Mankind. Armstrong knew instinctively what all great business communicators know—a pause at just the right time adds significance to words that the words themselves cannot express.

Great business communicators deliver their message with style. They know the impression they make often has less to do with the actual words they use than the way they deliver those words. Their tone, inflection, and speed, all serve to captivate their listeners.

★ ★ ★

Why am I dedicating an entire chapter to vocal delivery? Because it's more important than the actual words you use. You may have seen this statistic before, but it bears repeating: 55 percent of communication is visual (body language, eye contact); 38 percent is vocal (pitch, speed, volume variation); and only 7 percent of communication involves the actual words!

Preaching in the House of Cisco

In *The Eye of the Storm,* Robert Slater calls Cisco's John Chambers both a coach and a cheerleader. "The sheer explosiveness of his delivery gives the impression of a man racing, racing, racing, never willing to slow down. And he never does. He is an actor. He is a preacher. He is a coach. He is the head of the company. He is all those put together....Even if he were a dull speaker, the sales recruits would feel compelled to listen respectfully to their boss. But this man sweeping the audience is not dull. He is passionate and electrifying."

Passionate and electrifying. Imagine what your life would be like if people described you that way. I know you'll get closer to this goal once you identify and adopt all 10 Simple Secrets. But getting back to Chambers—he takes a cue from great anchors. He varies his delivery, speeding up and slowing down. His sentences are short, clean, and clear. His vocal delivery is impeccable, and as a result, he gets heard. One interesting note about Chambers—his voice is not deep like Cronkite or Brokaw and yet he is considered one of the great corporate speakers of our time. Don't get hung up on having a "broadcast voice." Most people who try to put on a deep baritone come off as affected, phony, and silly. This goes for inexperienced broadcast journalists as well. They try to be something they're not. In addition, contemporary audiences are evolving. Their tastes are changing. Contemporary listeners enjoy speakers who appear natural, not affected. Keep the focus on how you use the tools you've got instead of trying to change what doesn't come naturally.

Many years ago, a television network I worked for sent me to a voice coach who trained broadcasters. It was a benefit this network offered to all their new hires so I jumped at it. We spent a lot of time doing exercises to help me "get in touch with my instrument." This instructor also worked with corporate executives. I later picked up her book and found no reference to any contemporary communicators, but plenty of references to her background as an actress. That's the problem with most public speaking books—they're written by former actors and actresses who never got past summer stock in upstate New York. The reviews of this particular instructor's book told me all I needed to know—readers didn't see how her drills were relevant. Of course they didn't because the drills have nothing to do with their everyday presentations. You see, actors don't interview executives. If they did, they would find that most spokespeople don't have trouble with the quality of the voice but the way they use their voice to engage their audiences.

Delivering the Message at Full Throttle

Corporate leaders like Oracle CEO Larry Ellison make for good reading and keep newspaper columnists in business. Ellison is at times flamboyant, aggressive, and brilliant. The world's largest companies, including most banks and airlines, use Oracle's database. When you withdraw money at an ATM, there's a good chance Oracle's software is behind the scenes. When you make an airline reservation, Oracle's software is probably making it possible. It's everywhere. Oracle's success has rewarded investors who have seen the stock rise more than 40,000 percent since it went public in 1986 and it has made Ellison the fifth richest person in the world.

Ellison is a powerfully persuasive presenter. *PC Week* columnist, Jesse Berst, once described Ellison as having a rare combination of three qualities: technical depth, business savvy, and charisma. *Playboy* contributor, David Sheff, wrote that Ellison can "rally his troops with passion."

Ellison's speaking style is part of his charisma. His delivery is dazzling. Ellison is a master at using his voice to command the attention of his audiences during PowerPoint presentations, television interviews, or staff meetings. He's not afraid of using a dramatic pause. He speeds up and slows down. He pauses—one, two, three beats, or longer. He has a smooth, resonant voice. His delivery is casual, not contrived, engaging and energetic.

Here's a brief excerpt from an Ellison presentation in which he describes the benefits of "clustering," tying together large numbers of standard computers to do the same tasks as traditional supercomputers at a fraction of the cost. Ellison does so much with his voice in just a few sentences. Frankly, I can choose any two-minute section of the same presentation to demonstrate an example of Ellison's powerful delivery. This is as good as any. I used brackets to indicate gestures and changes in delivery speed. I also italicized the key words he emphasizes.

> Here's the second benefit of clusters [holds up two fingers]. In the old style, if you wanted to run faster [speeds up pace], then you bought a *larger* machine, and then a *larger* machine, and a larger machine. But what happens when you've spent all your money on the largest machine you can get? How do you go faster then? [pause] You can't. [pause] You can't. Unless, of course, you have *clusters* [speeds up]. Then instead of buying a larger machine, you simply buy another machine [pause], and another machine [pause], and another machine [pause], and another machine [pause]. It's performance on demand. There's *no limit* to performance.

Whether or not you care about "clusters" is beside the point. Ellison's audience does, even more so because his delivery grabs their attention. Like Chambers, Ellison is a corporate preacher, stirring the souls of his customers, employees, and investors. While his message is passionate, powerful, and clear, his spell-binding delivery and commanding body language contribute to his overall magnetism. By improving your delivery, you can do the same—mesmerizing your listeners.

Give That Man a Tony Award!

"Tony Blair is the most formidable communicator of the modern age," according to October 1, 2003, issue of London's *Independent*. While the UK has seen Blair rise to power over the years, Americans got their first real glimpse of him on a network called C-SPAN where they can watch his weekly defense of policies before the House of Commons. There are times I wish the American president had to face the same type of grilling. The House of Commons is a tough crowd. Even *Saturday Night Live* has poked fun at it.

The war in Iraq prompted a rare invitation for Blair to speak before a joint session of the U.S. Congress on July 17, 2003. Blair gave a dazzling presentation. While the words were beautifully written, his cadence, passion, and body language resonated with the American public. The next day, newspapers hailed the speech as a "passionate" defense of the Iraq war. Even critics of the U.S. administration and its war policies, like California senator Dianne Feinstein, said it was "the best speech I have ever heard." We're not here to debate the Iraq war. We're here to recognize that Blair is a powerful presenter. Period. We're here to identify and adopt the simple secrets behind his persuasive skills and magnetic speaking style. I know some of the speakers I've chosen to profile have made controversial statements. You'll love some of them, you'll hate others. But I think we can all agree they do an excellent job pitching their services, products, companies, or, in Blair's case, causes.

Philip Stephens is a senior correspondent for the *Financial Times*. He has covered politics in the UK, interviewed Blair extensively, and chronicled his rise to power in the book, *Tony Blair: The Making of a World Leader*. Stephens speaks directly to Blair's delivery style when he writes, "He stood out as a natural communicator. A young man with an instinctive ability to empathize with audiences, to strike just the right prose and cadence at just the right moment."

Blair struck the right chord during the funeral for Princess Diana. Hundreds of millions of people watched as Blair, only in office for a few months, perfectly captured the emotions of the nation. Blair said Diana was "The People's Princess [pause] that is how she will stay, how she will remain in our hearts and memories forever." About that speech, Stephens writes, "The words were perfectly delivered, the voice breaking at precisely the right moment, the grief etched on the prime minister's face."

Blair commands an audience because he makes sure the way he delivers his words matches the impact of the words themselves. Make no mistake; he's very conscious of it. Blair is very careful with the words, phrases, and delivery of his presentations. As prime minister, Blair has access to a ton of speechwriters, but he prefers to work on many of the speeches himself. Why? Because he writes for the ear.

Write for the Ear

Peggy Noonan wrote some of the most memorable phrases in recent history while working as a speechwriter for Ronald Reagan and George Bush Sr. In her book, *Simply Speaking,* Noonan reinforces the importance of keeping sentences short and easy to say, especially sentences written to be read aloud. Long sentences are more difficult to read because "you'll run out of breath, emphasize the wrong word, trail off."

Most of what you say starts with what you write. Captivating speakers start with the end in mind: their delivery. Patricia Dean is the associate director of the prestigious Annenberg School of Journalism at USC. We met when I was a student at Northwestern—Dean ran the broadcast program at the Medill School of Journalism. Many of the great broadcast journalists you see on TV are Pat Dean's protégés. As an instructor, she's tops. According to Dean, "Great television anchors know the scripts must be written for the ear and the scripts must be comfortable for them to deliver. Awkward phrasing and complicated sentences are difficult to read and make it difficult, if not impossible, for the audience to follow. A dull, monotone delivery will destroy even the most brilliant speech."

One of Dean's favorite speakers is poet Maya Angelou. Angelou has been hailed as one of the great "voices" of contemporary literature.

Angelou's words are stunning but the words come alive with Angelou's powerful delivery. Although she has a string of best-selling books like *I Know Why the Caged Bird Sings,* Angelou's popularity soared when she read one of her poems, "On the Pulse of Morning," for President Bill Clinton's inauguration in 1993. The poem's words, about hope and survival, were beautifully written but until that day most people had just read her poems. Angelou brought a completely new dimension to her work by the way she used her voice. Newspaper articles written the day after the inauguration praised Angelou for her "hypnotic presence" and her "powerful delivery" that left as deep an impression as her words.

You're not going to enter your next staff meeting delivering your presentation in the same deliberative, thoughtful, and dramatic fashion as Angelou reads her poetry. But there is something we can all learn from Angelou. She pauses at key moments, punches key words, and varies her tone and inflection to make her words come alive. Angelou has a magnetic presence because she loves language and takes great care with the words she chooses, how they sound, and how they're delivered. She teaches us that both the words we use and the way we say those words are critical to captivating our listeners.

What Great Anchors Know That You Don't

Jennings. Brokaw. Cronkite. Wallace. Those names are the reason I enrolled in a broadcast Master's program. During college, I recall rushing home after class to catch ABC's *World News Tonight with Peter Jennings.* What a geek I must have been. I also read *Vital Speeches,* which had nothing to do with my classes. Let's move on before I destroy any hope of ever being remembered as a cool guy on campus.

Jennings has a great voice, but it's the way he uses his voice that makes him pleasing on the ear. The next time you watch him, listen to his pace. It's rapid, but not too fast. He varies his inflections. Every syllable is clear and understandable. Jennings also adds emphasis to the most important words in the paragraph, and he slows down to highlight key concepts. Jennings, like all great broadcasters, draws you in to the stories he tells.

In *Put Your Best Foot Forward,* famed jury consultant Jo-Ellan Dimitrius writes, "The broadcast media have spent millions of dollars searching for the perfect voice. They have found that the ideal voice must show emotion, be lower pitched, be moderately paced, and…it must be free of distracting qualities, clear, and have moderate volume." Dimitrius has discovered that this "ideal" voice is proven to be the most persuasive among jurors. Jurors tend to like people with these vocal qualities. You're goal is to be liked. It's hard to persuade anybody of anything if they don't like you first. Your voice, and the way you use it, has a lot to do with it. I find that most spokespeople have perfectly fine voices but, unlike Jennings, they don't use it effectively. It's like keeping a Ferrari parked in the garage. Drive it every once in awhile!

A Stunning Landscape Portrait

Broadcast news professionals work for years on their voice. You don't have to. In fact, five simple techniques will help you significantly improve your delivery style for your next meeting, speech, pitch, or presentation. Adopt these techniques to turn your next presentation into a broadcast quality event.

1. Tone It Up
2. Pick Up the Pace
3. Pause…for Impact
4. Punch Key Words
5. Cross Your Ts

Tone It Up

Remember the description of former California governor as being a "monotone" speaker? That means he didn't have any inflection in his voice or changes in the pitch and tone of his voice. Monotone is dull. It's uninspiring. It's deadly. A monotone speaker strings words and phrases together in the same tone of voice—a dull, repetitive style of sound. It's great for Tibetan chants when you're trying to sleep, but you want your listeners to stay alert for your entire presentation. Your voice should be like a stunning landscape portrait with peaks and valleys, variations in pitch, volume, and inflections. Your voice should rise and fall, curve, twist, and turn. It'll mesmerize your listeners and leave them with a sense of awe.

★ ★ ★

Some business leaders can get away with a monotone delivery. Terry Semel is CEO of Yahoo! An article in the April 2004 issue of *Fortune* described him this way: "In front of a big crowd, his Brooklyn-accented monotone made most people's eyes glaze. Silicon Valley, home to Oracle's Larry Ellison, Apple's Steve Jobs, and Sun Microsystems' Scott McNealy, likes its CEOs on the flamboyant side." There's one difference between Terry Semel and you. He co-headed Warner Brothers and is considered one of the most successful business leaders in Hollywood. Semel has done a sensational job at Yahoo! and is one of the great business leaders of our time. But his accomplishments and vision command attention, not his delivery style. He's obviously okay with that. You can't afford to be. The last thing you should want is to be described as a speaker who makes people's eyes "glaze over." It could stop your career dead in its tracks, long before you build a reputation that commands attention for your accomplishments alone.

Pick Up the Pace

I've come to believe the world's greatest business communicators speak a little faster than average. I discovered this early in my career when I compared my rate of speech with broadcast journalists like Peter Jennings. He read the same copy at a little faster pace than I did. And he sounded better. The average American speaks at a rate of 125 to 150 words per minute (wpm). Jennings, by comparison, speaks at a rate closer to 200 wmp.

This is enormously important. I find that very few people in my seminars speak too fast. Most of them have just the opposite problem—they talk way too slow. It's like watching sap drip from a tree. The last thing you want to be is a sap. If your listeners are tuning out, or looking at their watch during your presentation, it's quite possible your rate of speech is too slow.

Even research shows that listeners prefer a rate of speech that's a bit faster than average. In the January 2001 issue of the *International Journal of Instructional Media,* a study found "speeded spokespersons were perceived as more knowledgeable, enthusiastic, and more energetic than those speaking at normal speed." The study did find that comprehension "declined precipitously" past 250 wpm but few people speak anywhere close to that rate. Please don't try!

Broadcasters like Jennings aren't the only ones with a faster than average rate of speech. I've analyzed both Apple CEO Steve Jobs and Cisco CEO John Chambers. During live presentations they speak anywhere from 190 to 195 wpm approximately. I'll tell you what's really amazing about this—they're both using PowerPoint and discussing the material on the slides. But they are such masters of the material there are no awkward breaks in the flow of their delivery. That's the key—become a master of delivery. I think what happens to most of us, while we're presenting, is that we slow down to process the information. We're thinking about what comes next. Perhaps we're not as prepared as we should be. Others tend to be nervous which also slows them down. But when you've mastered the material, internalized it, and feel comfortable, confident, and powerful, the words flow more easily.

Pause...for Impact

Speaking before the House of Commons two days after the terrorist attacks on the World Trade Center September 11, 2001, Tony Blair vowed to help the United States fight terrorism worldwide. Blair knows a pause at just the right time will convey an enormity and seriousness to his words. He saved his longest pause before and after this sentence: "One thing should be very clear. Those that harbor or help terrorists will have a choice—either to cease their protection of our enemies—or be treated as an enemy themselves."

You don't have to be a head of state to leverage the power of a dramatic pause. Glance back at the Larry Ellison transcript earlier in the chapter. He uses pauses more frequently, and with greater impact, than most business presenters I've seen. Here's a brief quote from a television interview I saw with Ellison. I added the pauses in brackets:

> You can't conform in business. You have to be very careful. If you adhere to conventional wisdom [pause] if you do everything everyone else does in business [pause] you're going to lose. The only way to get ahead [pause] to really get ahead [pause] is to be different.

Ellison uses dramatic pauses to draw listeners into his conversation. He'll often use the pause to set off his key points, to "flag" it, so to speak, as if to say, what I'm about to tell you is very important so listen up! If you use pauses effectively, like Ellison, you'll get people to listen up as well. Coupling these pauses with direct and confident eye contact will really take your presentations to the next level (but that would be jumping ahead to Simple Secret #8).

After Hewlett Packard acquired Compaq, then-CEO Carly Fiorina sat down for a Q&A session in front of a packed house at Silicon Valley's Commonwealth Club. Fiorina was asked how she managed to stay focused during the grueling takeover battle: "You have to rely on that compass. [pause] Who am I? [pause] What do I believe? [pause] Do I believe we're doing the right things for the right reasons and the right ways [pause] and sometimes that's all you have."

Fiorina continues:

> Leadership is all about enabling people to achieve more than they thought was possible. [pause] Leadership is all about seeing potential and possibility. [pause] Management is also about fixing weaknesses and shoring up problems. But it can't just be about that. [pause] It has to be about possibility, potential, and aspiration. A lot of what a leader does is to unlock the potential that exists in an organization and to build lasting capability for the business to move ahead.

Your job as a speaker is to "unlock" the potential of your presentation by respecting its words enough to take a breath every once in a while so your audience can soak in the message. Actor Jim Carrey once said, "Constantly talking isn't necessarily communicating." Good advice. Sometimes taking a breath will breathe life into your presentations.

If you want to hear an effective use of the pause, watch actor Martin Sheen on NBC's *The West Wing*. As President Josiah Bartlett, Sheen can deliver a speech better than most real-life politicians or executive leaders. The writers are brilliant but Sheen's timing and pauses work magic with the words.

Punch Key Words

Fox News Channel's Stuart Varney has spent decades in front of a television camera and as a popular keynote speaker. The key to delivering his message with maximum impact, he tells me, is to "punch" or stress the key words in each sentence. "Like a machine gun," says Varney.

I watched one speech Varney gave to a group of business professionals in 2003. Like all good presenters, after some friendly banter, Varney began the substance of his talk by outlining the major points he was going to make. Here are his exact words. I italicized the words he chose to emphasize in each sentence.

I want to make *three* points. First, I want to look at the *state* of the U.S. economy *right now*. Believe me, the timing of this meeting is absolutely superb because in my view the *future* of the U.S. economy depends very much on the *outcome* of the war that is now in progress in Iraq. So I want to discuss *where* we are now, *how* we got here, and *where* this U.S. economy is going. I'm an optimist. I believe we are shortly about to embark on a new period of expansion in the U.S. economy. Secondly, I want to discuss what I call the *new structure* of the global economy because it has shifted and changed *quite dramatically* in recent years. It's my opinion that we now have what I'm going to call a *bi-polar* global economy. That is, the United States of America as the great *consumer* and China as the great *maker*, the workshop of the world. These are now the two poles of this new global economy. It is now a bi-polar global economy with *enormous implications* for international diplomacy, international business and international economics. *Thirdly,* I'm going to talk about *fertility rates* (laughs). This is not going to be a boring speech on economics. I'm going to talk about fertility rates today because throughout the developed world, all of a sudden fertility rates have *declined very, very sharply*. We're at the point where it is noticeable in thirty or forty countries that the population is declining, declining *rapidly*. It is the exact *opposite* of what we were expecting just a few short years ago when the world's population was predicted to *explode forever*. We're not being swamped. In fact, fertility rates have reached the point where we have declining populations in many countries in the developed world. And if you *think* about it, can you imagine what kind of *profound effect* it will have on our standard of living, our *economic* life and our *business* life. It has a profound effect when your population starts to *shrink*. That's what I'm going to talk about.

Can you see how punching the key word or words in your sentences will help you develop a delivery that's more engaging than a boring, dull monotone? Hit those key words. Here are some examples:

- We can help you reduce your IT spending by *fifty percent*!
- *Now* is the time for action!
- I need *your* help to accomplish this goal. *Together,* we will *revolutionize* the industry and *change the world!*

Varney's machine gun delivery may not be the only reason he's paid an enormous amount of money to give a speech, but his knack for punching the key words adds to his magnetism in public and on television.

Cross Your Ts

There's a hilarious episode of *Seinfeld* when the character George Costanza brings his girlfriend to meet Jerry, Elaine, and Kramer. The episode is called "The Low Talker" because everyone strains to hear every word the girlfriend says. Of course, they misinterpret every word, landing Costanza in hot water and costing him yet another relationship. I think there's a vocal quality that's just as bad—The Mumbler!

I used to get my car's oil changed at a place close to my home. My wife makes sure it never goes three thousand miles without it. I guess it works as one of our cars has over two hundred fifty thousand miles on it and it's still going strong! A short time ago, I stopped going to this particular oil changer, which was not "quick" as its named implied. But I stopped giving them business, not because it wasn't fast, but because I couldn't understand a word the new manager said. He mumbled everything.

The first time I simply asked to replace the oil and filter. I think he recommended some other services but I couldn't tell. So I left it at a simple oil change. After another three thousand miles, I decided to give him a second chance. You never know, I thought, maybe it was especially loud as other cars were being worked on. The same thing happened. With several oil change shops within two miles of this place, I took my business elsewhere. I honestly didn't think this book would apply to a manager of an oil change business, but it proved to me that "presentations" happen every day, in every industry, in every field.

Great business communicators clearly enunciate every word. You can make out everything they say. The king of enunciation is ABC's Peter Jennings. Next time you see him, close your eyes and listen to the words. You can hear every consonant. He doesn't trail off at the end of sentences. Mumbling is one of the easiest mistakes to correct. You just need to be aware of it as you listen to yourself on tape or on a phone's voice message. The problem most speakers have is failing to pronounce final consonants in words that end in "NT." Most people simply trail off, so words like "can't" sound like "can" and words like "won't" sounds like "won." These are fairly simple problems to overcome. At the beginning of my career, I certainly would not have received an A for articulation. Believe it or not, reciting simple tongue twisters improved my enunciation. When I watch one of my stories repeated on videotape, and I catch myself falling into bad habits, I simply recite one of the many tongue twisters you'll find in the Coaching Drills of this chapter. They work!

★ ★ ★

Barbara Corcoran works on the quality of her delivery. Corcoran told me that she advises people to tape themselves to hear how they come across on the phone, or listen to themselves on a message machine.

"So much in business, how you meet people, is by phone. The first impression is so powerful, why would you not be careful with how you come across on the phone? Ninety percent of what I do is on the phone. Step outside yourself to hear how you come across. By listening to yourself, you hear your enunciation and tone. I always suggest to my salespeople, if they're not 150 percent confident, stand up while they're on the phone. It comes across. It makes a huge difference."

By now I hope you're convinced that how you deliver your message is equally as important as the words themselves. Keep your listeners engaged by using all of the techniques of great business and broadcast speakers—varying your tone, inflections, speed, using pauses to set aside key thoughts and phrases, punching important words, and enunciating clearly. Remember, your words are like a stunning landscape portrait, not a concrete wall in a warehouse.

Your magnificent delivery has pulled your audience in deeper. Let's take it up another level. It's time to reveal the eighth Simple Secret of all great business communicators.

1. **Take a Lesson from the Masters.** Visit this book's website, www.carminegallo.com, for more profiles and video links to master communicators. Listen carefully as they make their words come alive with their tone, pitch, inflection, emphasis, and pauses. Notice how no two sentences are delivered exactly alike!

2. **Written for the Ear.** Read the headline and the first few paragraphs of the big news story of the day in the *New York Times, Washington Post,* or *Los Angeles Times.* They are typically not written for the ear. Then, compare the headline and opening sentences of the same story in *USA Today.* The writing in *USA Today* is much closer to broadcast style than you might think. Try reading both out loud. Which is easier? Which sounds more natural? Next, pay attention to how television news anchors deliver that very same story. They'll use shorter words and shorter sentences. They'll vary their tone and inflections while emphasizing key words.

3. **Tongue Twisters.** Tape yourself reading these tongue twisters. Is every word distinguishable? Keep practicing and build your speed until you can enunciate every word as you read them rapidly:

A BIG BLACK BUG BIT A BIG BLACK BEAR MADE A BIG BLACK BEAR BLEED.

PETER PIPER PICKED A PECK OF PICKLED PEPPERS. IF PETER PIPER PICKED A PECK OF PICKLED PEPPERS, WHERE IS THE PECK OF PICKLED PEPPERS PETER PIPER PICKED?

IF A WOODCHUCK WOULD CHUCK WOOD, HOW MUCH WOOD WOULD A WOODCHUCK CHUCK, IF A WOODCHUCK WOULD? BUT IF A WOODCHUCK WOULD CHUCK WOOD, HOW MUCH WOOD WOULD A WOODCHUCK CHUCK, IF A WOODCHUCK COULD AND WOULD CHUCK WOOD?

SIMPLE SECRET #8: COMMAND PRESENCE

MOVEMENT DOES A BODY GOOD

"When we asked 125 adults what most impressed them that a person was confident, the person's body language was mentioned more than twice as frequently as any other category."

JURY CONSULTANT JO-ELLAN DIMITRIUS

Justin Sullivan/Getty Images

"A company is people–people with brains and hearts and guts. If you're a leader, you've got to capture the whole person. People want to see you get it intellectually and feel it emotionally."

FORMER HEWLETT PACKARD CEO
CARLY FIORINA

Some presentations are more important than others. There are some in which failure could cost your job, your reputation, and your company. One of my clients, a top executive for a technology firm, was preparing to give a major presentation to the company's primary investor—a famous CEO who is one of the wealthiest men in the world. Let's call the investor Big Dog. In addition to positive news about the product, its patents, and engineering milestones, my client also had to address an uncomfortable fact—they had hit a snag in the development and would have to delay the launch of the product.

That presented a slight problem—his body language. Everything about it said, "We're in deep trouble. We don't have a clue as to how to solve this glitch and the delay might very well become permanent. I'm lost. I can't lead this team and your money won't last as long as J.Lo's first marriage." Of course, that wasn't the case at all. Far from it. In fact, my client's engineering team had jumped far greater hurdles in the past. They were all very confident the current stall would easily be overcome and the product would go on to become a smashing success (which it eventually did).

I watched as this executive rehearsed his PowerPoint presentation. The content on the slides wasn't the problem; the problem was with the spokesman delivering the content. My client spoke volumes with what he didn't say. His body language was a mess—eyes cast downward, hands awkwardly tucked in his pockets, swaying back and forth. This guy was a poster boy for poor body language. He seemed insecure and out of his league. Oh, there's one thing I neglected to mention about Big Dog. In addition to being a demanding investor, he's also one of the top CEOs in the world and a dazzling presenter in his own right. Since my client's performance could very well have doomed his career, I took a drastic "tough love" measure and decided to show him a videotape of Big Dog giving a rousing presentation to a standing-room crowd. I said, "This is what you're being compared to." My client got the hint quickly.

Fortunately, this story has a good ending. In addition to working on each of the other 10 Simple Secrets in the book, my client eliminated bad habits and rocked the house during his presentation. He made solid eye contact with everybody in the room, he pulled his hands out of his pockets and used purposeful, assertive hand gestures. His posture and stance exuded power, confidence, and competence—he had charisma! In fact, I heard later that Big Dog turned to the firm's CEO to say he was pleased with the presentation and expressed confidence the project was in good hands. Big Dog was happy and my client could happily continue to show up at the office.

Quick follow-up: my client really didn't want to give this particular presentation for obvious reasons, but his boss thought he would be the best spokesperson as he understood the problem better than anyone. He understood the issue better than anyone in the firm and was one of the top experts in the field. But his presentations would suffer until he believed he belonged on the stage. Well, this executive has built up so much confidence after the success of his Big Dog presentation I'm told he volunteers to speak for nearly every situation. There's only one problem—his boss recently told me—they need an umbrella to drag him off the stage. Now that my client has mastered Simple Secret #8, it seems to me I'd better send him Simple Secret #6 on brevity!

Command Presence

The world's greatest business communicators have great body language—a commanding presence that reflects confidence, competence, and charisma. Command Presence is a military term to describe someone who presents him or herself as a person with authority, someone to be respected and followed. It's how you talk, how you walk, and how you look. How much would people sacrifice to follow you? Would they leave a high-paying job, good benefits, and a life-long pension? If so, you have command presence.

Commander Matt Eversmann has it. His body language is impeccable. His back is straight—no slouching for this soldier. He maintains eye contact with the audience. He uses appropriate hand gestures. "What role does body language, or command presence, play in the development of a leader?" I asked Eversmann.

Eversmann believes it's second only to passion in importance. "Do you look, act, talk, and walk like a person people want to follow when things get rough?" Eversmann asks.

> Great leaders have an air of confidence. Subordinates need to look up to somebody who is still standing strong, like an oak, regardless of events around them. You need to convey a feeling that you will always be in control despite the circumstances, even if you don't have an immediate solution. As someone who doesn't lose focus, doesn't cower, doesn't waffle. The air of confidence must come out.

Do you have the air of confidence in the corporate battlefield? Great communicators do. A leader who fails to instill confidence among his subordinates—during hundreds of everyday actions—will lose the loyalty of his "troops" when it really counts. In her book, *Put Your Best Foot Forward,* famed jury consultant Jo-Ellan Dimitrius addresses body language stereotypes: "People believe that those who have good posture have the capability to lead, they're self confident, interested, and honest."

American Idol Syndrome

Great business communicators know that words alone will not rally their audiences. They use strong, confident body language to add polish to their presentations, speeches, or meetings. **Good** business communicators understand the concept, but don't put it into practice as much as they should. **Average** business communicators need a friendly reminder. **Poor** business communicators—dull, uninspiring, and painful to watch—are completely oblivious to their lack of skill. But of course they think they're great! I call it the *American Idol* Syndrome. After interviewing the world's top spokespeople for more than fifteen years in television, I've noticed a correlation: those who say they're great presenters or spokespeople are inevitably the worst. Those who are more modest, and who ask for feedback, are by far the best. Don't ask me to explain it. I'm a journalist not a therapist!

★ ★ ★

In the April 2001 issue of the *Harvard Management Communication Letter,* speechwriter Nick Morgan argues for what he calls a kinesthetic speaker who "feeds an audience's essentially primal hunger to experience a presentation on a physical, as well as an intellectual level. Through an awareness of their own physical presence—their gestures, posture, and presentation, kinesthetic speakers can create potent nonverbal messages that are consistent with and reinforce their verbal ones."

Be a Confident Self-Promoter

Tory Johnson, founder and CEO of Women for Hire, tells me that paying attention to body language is especially important for women who want to win over recruiters or bosses.

"How you carry yourself is critical," says Johnson.

Especially in person, a visual first impression is often more powerful than what you say. With women, often there is a discomfort with self-promotion. For example, women tend to downplay their successes. They shy away from their accomplishments much more so than men. They are nervous about coming across as conceited, a show-off, or a braggart. It's reflected in the language they use and their body language: averting their eyes, not standing tall, not having a firm handshake, not smiling. A simple fix is to recognize that being a confident self-promoter is perfectly acceptable and in fact necessary in the job search process. The things you say about yourself and the confidence with which you say them are going to take you far in the job search process and often is the differentiating factor between one candidate and another.

I would argue it's also the differentiating factor between a great corporate spokesperson and an average one! Now, more than ever, the jobs of many American workers are dispensable. They're being shipped overseas by the hundreds of thousands. At the same time more people are graduating from college and getting advanced degrees. Competition is tough for the top jobs. Stand apart by carrying yourself as a standout.

Break the Barrier

The advent of around-the-clock business news coverage on cable networks like CNBC, CNN, and the Fox News channel has redefined the relationship investors have with executive leaders. A closeness has inadvertently occurred that requires a new way of looking at business communications— one of the reasons why I consider a discussion of Greek orators largely irrelevant to twenty-first century presentations—especially as it relates to body language.

Powerful body language is one of the secrets behind John Chambers's reputation as a dazzling corporate presenter. His body language is part of his charisma. Chambers has become a master at getting close to his audience by breaking the physical barrier that separates him and his listeners. It's a technique that helps him establish trust with his audience. He is so skilled that most people think it comes naturally. His expressive, emotional, and optimistic nature may have come naturally but his presentation style has evolved over time.

During one of our conversations, I asked Cisco vice president of corporate positioning Ron Ricci, "How has Chambers improved as a presenter, specifically as it relates to his body language?"

"Over eight years, he's evolved by working the audience and breaking the barrier," says Ricci.

> One of the things he's developed is this idea of walking through the crowd, looking them in the eye, putting his hand on their shoulder, and asking them questions. He wasn't that way in the beginning. Although he's always been personable, this evangelical quality—putting his hands on individuals—is an evolved capacity. He gets off the stage to remind people that he's the message, not the PowerPoint. That's his thing. Get away from the podium. He's got that "Baptist minister" quality. His audience is his flock and he's there to get them to focus on the opportunity. He believes you should treat people like you want to be treated yourself. Well, the way he wants to be treated is to have somebody have a personal conversation with him. He doesn't want you to feel as though you're one of five hundred people in the audience. He wants you to feel like you're having a one-on-one conversation with him. The eye contact, putting a hand on a shoulder, high-fives, asking them questions, he does all those things.

Chambers breaks the barrier without saying a word.

WARNING—Don't touch people during your next presentation! Chambers is a skilled speaker who has worked on his techniques for years. Yes, he's even had formal coaching. He knows what he's doing. When he "touches" people, it's literally a light hand, briefly placed on someone's shoulder. And he uses the technique rarely and precisely. I'm afraid you'll misinterpret Ricci's observation and go nuts during your next meeting, speech, or presentation—which might be your last at your company. Here's the point: great business communicators, like Chambers, don't simply stand behind a podium with their hands in their pockets. They use their bodies effectively to break down the barrier between speaker and listener—creating a closeness and trust—while inspiring confidence in themselves and their message.

Every January, 2,000 political, academic, media, and business leaders gather for the World Economic Forum in Davos, Switzerland for five days of workshops and speeches on global challenges. More than 125 leaders spoke at the 2004 conference including former President Bill Clinton, Vice President Dick Cheney, and New York financier George Soros. According to *Fast Company,* "John Chambers went toe to toe with global heavies at the 2004 World Economic Forum in Davos, Switzerland. High-level debate on global economics isn't normally within a corporate CEO's zone of comfort. But at Davos, Chambers's persuasive oratory stole the show." My goal is to help you steal the show! And there are plenty of shows to be stolen. Don't let someone else beat you to it!

Zero to Sixty in Three Steps

Great business communicators pay attention to their words as well as to what their body language is saying. Both speak volumes. Your body language must reflect your confidence, passion, and know-how. Unfortunately, when it comes to body language, I'm afraid corporate spokespeople might suffer from information overload. A quick Internet search for books on "body language" turned up more than one hundred thousand results! My gosh—how many ways are there to read facial expressions? One book promises to make anyone fall in love with me. I don't think my wife would appreciate that advice. Another promises to help improve my relationship with my cat by "reading" my cat's body language. My cat and I get along just fine, thank you.

Here's the problem—the science of body language and the volumes of books dedicated to the subject could distract you from the very simple steps you can take to turbo-charge your presentations. Remember Big Dog and the executive at the beginning of this chapter? Some very simple changes in his posture resulted in a much more confident, persuasive, and dynamic presentation. I've seen presenters go from zero to sixty in less than an hour, simply by adopting the following three techniques shared by the world's greatest business communicators:

1. Open Posture
2. Eye Contact
3. Hand Gestures

Open for Business

"Slumped, casual, or loose body posture is associated not only with a lack of self-confidence, leadership ability, and interest, but also with a lack of attention to detail, and hence reflects poorly on reliability and capability," writes Jo-Ellan Dimitrius in *Put Your Best Foot Forward*. She should know. Dimitrius gets paid millions of dollars to read the body language of potential jurors in major trials. Dimitrius has one of the simplest explanations for open posture. It boils down to this—don't put anything between you and the listener. Recall how Chambers walks away from a podium? Podiums are out (although sometimes you can't avoid them since there's only one microphone, and it's attached to the stand). But there are many simple ways of keeping an open posture in meetings, sales calls, or virtually any type of presentation:

If You:	Then:
Hold objects in front of you	Put them down
Cross your arms	Uncross them
Keep your hands in your pockets	Take them out

These very common habits are easy to fix. Anytime you place anything between you and the listener, you create a barrier, an unconscious defensive mechanism that indicates you're hiding something—whether you are or not. But it registers in the mind of your listeners. According to Dimitrius, it makes you appear to be less reliable, honest, and confident. So the simple fix—remove the obstacles. Now you're open for business!

In Your Eyes, the Light, the Heat

Remember the Peter Gabriel song "In Your Eyes"? It became famous as part of the soundtrack to the '80s movie *Say Anything*. The song has a powerful anti-apartheid message. Even Nelson Mandela requested that Gabriel play the song for a major fund-raising concert in South Africa. Notice that Peter Gabriel doesn't feel "the light, the heat" in your hands, or in you ears. It's in the eyes—the simplest vehicle through which to establish a powerful connection with your listeners.

★ ★ ★

A study discussed in the *Journal of Services Marketing* found bank tellers who used more eye contact were rated more highly in customer satisfaction surveys. The satisfaction carried over to the way customers rated the bank itself. Can you picture the success you'll enjoy if your audience rated your service, product, company, or cause highly based on your powerful body language and eye contact?

Eye contact is associated with honesty, trustworthiness, sincerity, confidence—all the traits you strive for on your way to becoming a great business communicator. We like people who look us in the eye. Period. Whether speaking to large groups or one-on-one, eye contact is critical. This is the main reason preparation (Simple Secret #3) is so important, so we can avoid breaking that contact to read from notes or slides. But how long should you maintain eye contact? After all, gazing directly into someone's eyes too long makes people uncomfortable. You need to build in natural breaks. Dimitrius says most people maintain eye contact 40 to 70 percent of the time, but she suggests you will have the most "positive impact" if you maintain eye contact 60 to 70 percent of the time. For more professional situations, Dimitrius says 70 to 80 percent is appropriate without appearing too intense. One of the best pieces of advice I've heard is to maintain eye contact long enough to register the color of your listener's eyes.

When speaking to larger groups, great communicators make everyone feel as though they're talking directly to each individual. Fox News Channel's Stuart Varney scans the audience. "I constantly move my attention to different parts of the room, from the extreme right to the center to the extreme left. I look at different parts of the room to draw everyone into the conversation. I make everyone feel as though I'm talking to them, not at them. I'm not lecturing, but conversing, as we would be doing at a dinner party." How would you feel if the person you're speaking to at a dinner party has her back turned to you or he's looking at the blonde over your shoulder? It's not very engaging, is it?

★ ★ ★

"Carmine, if you've been to a presentation where people look down at prepared notes, the energy just ebbs out of their performance. If you can't see someone's eyes, the presentation falls flat."
Martin Gagen, venture capitalist

Italians Are on to Something

I'm Italian. That means I use my hands—a lot. I think it's a requirement of being full-blooded Italian. I'm proud of the Italian contribution to our culture. Some of the greatest leaders, inventors, artists, and athletes have been Italian. We've even contributed to pop culture with HBO's Tony Soprano. Great business communicators have adopted one of our most common habits—using our hands! Hand gestures, used sparingly and appropriately, can energize a presentation.

I've spent some long conversations with a man whose pioneering research should be far more visible in the field of leadership and communications. So let's give him his due because it will help transform you into a powerful presenter. Dr. David McNeill at the University of Chicago is known for his exhaustive research in the area of hand gestures. He's made it his passion since 1980. His research has shown that gestures and language are intimately connected. In fact, the use of gestures can help presenters speak better by clearing up their thought process. Yes, he says, it actually takes concentrated effort NOT to use gestures and "takes away from the rest of your mental capacities."

Dr. McNeill has found that very disciplined, rigorous, and confident thinkers use hand gestures that reflect the clarity of their thinking, a "window to their thought process." His favorite examples include President Bill Clinton, British prime minister Tony Blair, Secretary of State Colin Powell, and Donald Rumsfeld (defense secretary in the George W. Bush administration). Simply by watching the gestures they make, McNeill can tell that each of these speakers has a methodical, disciplined, and rigorous way of thinking. By reflecting clear thinking, the gestures they use instill confidence in their listeners—although most people would not immediately attribute their magnetism as speakers to the way they use their hands. That's a powerful concept because so few presenters get it. (My mother certainly gets it. I can tell exactly what she's saying just by watching her hands!) By understanding the power of hand gestures, it can help you stand apart.

★ ★ ★

I had to think twice about using Donald Rumsfeld as an example in this book. At the time of this writing, with the Iraq war still as contentious as ever, Rumsfeld was a lightening rod for criticism. As secretary of defense, he was responsible for strategic actions taken after the terrorist attacks of September 11, 2001. He promoted a much more aggressive foreign policy action, including the invasion of Iraq in March 2003. He was a polarizing figure in the U.S. and around the world, but that shouldn't detract from our observations of him as a speaker. Rumsfeld was the CEO of two *Fortune* 500 companies. Like the other personalities in this book, there's no mistaking a simple fact—he has command presence, in abundance.

A couple of days after my conversation with Dr. McNeill regarding hand gestures, I watched Rumsfeld as he defended his policies during a press conference. Wouldn't you know it, Dr. McNeill was absolutely right. Rumsfeld complimented virtually every sentence with an emphatic gesture. And he made his gestures above-the-waist, which is more powerful. He varied his gestures—sometimes one hand, sometimes two hands. He would use his fingers to list specific results, he clenched his fists to show resolve, and he kept both his palms open when discussing the need for unity and "joint operations." He was engaging, dynamic, forceful, confident, and strong—all the qualities of a great presenter.

Here's the challenge. I can't tell you what kind of gestures to make. Neither can McNeill. Rumsfeld, Powell, or Chambers don't consciously think to themselves, "Now I'm going to make this gesture." The minute you try to copy a hand gesture, you risk looking contrived—like a bad politician. Worse yet, you might look like a joke. President George Bush Sr. used gestures that were often incongruous with his words, as if he had been over-coached. It was like mismatched audio in a bad B movie. Dana Carvey made a career out of impersonating Bush, distracting hand gestures and all, on *Saturday Night Live*. The last thing you want is for your colleagues to make fun of you after a meeting.

★ ★ ★

Speaking of contrived gestures, I think "steepling" should be outlawed. This is the gesture people make by aligning the fingers of both hands together in the form of a steeple. Somewhere down the line somebody said it conveys superiority and confidence. It's now so overused it looks phony, like you're trying to convey something you're not. Look, if it comes naturally then do it every once in awhile. But I recall an interview with a top CEO who held the steeple pose for several minutes. After the interview a producer asked me, "Why did that guy hold his hands like that? How odd!" Don't be odd. Be natural.

Based on conversations with McNeill, here are three simple pieces of advice that will help you use hand gestures more effectively:

1. Use gestures

Don't be afraid to use your hands in the first place! The second worst piece of speaking advice, after "start with a joke," is to keep your hands at your sides. Who came up with that one? "Actors never leave gestures to chance," says McNeill. That partially explains why Schwarzenegger's body language was so effective when compared to former California governor Gray Davis in the November 2002 California gubernatorial election. As you'll recall from our discussion of Simple Secret #2, an analysis of newspapers articles revealed that Davis was described as stiff, wooden, or robotic while Schwarzenegger was described as commanding or charismatic. Davis's hand gestures were often unconnected to his words, almost as an after-thought. All great business speakers use hand gestures that are appropriate to the content of their message. Don't be afraid to use them. The simplest fix for a "stiff" presentation is simply to pull your hands out of your pockets—and to use them!

2. Use gestures sparingly

Okay, now that I've told you to use hand gestures I'm going to suggest you don't use them that much! McNeill urges caution. Don't go overboard. Too many gestures at each and every point in your presentation will make it seem as though you're stepping in as traffic cop at a big-city intersection. That leads to the final piece of advice.

3. Use gestures at key moments

McNeill has found that great speakers are more inclined to use definitive and purposeful gestures during "key moments in the discourse." In other words, if it's important, use your hands to reinforce the point. We learned from Simple Secret #7 that key words need to be emphasized, like a machine gun. Your hands are bullets, too. Shoot them at the right time.

★ ★ ★

In 1991, General Norman Schwarzkopf led the U.S. and its allies in Operation Desert Storm to move Saddam Hussein and his forces out of Kuwait. He's credited for bringing the ground war to a close in just four days. When it was over, *ABC News* took the unprecedented step of airing Schwarzkopf's entire press conference explaining the military tactics that brought an end to the war. It was brilliant. Schwarzkopf was praised for his clarity and his powerfully commanding presence. When a reporter asked Schwarzkopf for his assessment of Saddam Hussein as a military leader, Schwarzkopf leaned in, took a dramatic pause, and used his fingers, one at a time, to list each observation in the following summary: "As far as Saddam Hussein being a great military strategist, he is neither a strategist, nor is he schooled in the operational arts, nor is he a tactician, nor is he a general, nor is he a soldier. Other than that, he's a great military man. I want you to know that." He used gestures to reinforce the "key moment of his discourse."

The Single Greatest Tool to Study Hand Gestures

The biggest challenge I have discussing hand gestures is describing how great presenters use them. Words and drawings can't do justice to how gestures can enhance a message. So why try? That's why the Internet is one of the most powerful tools for contemporary corporate speakers; it allows you to visit a website and watch streaming presentations of dazzling corporate spokespeople. It's another reason why I don't care much for public-speaking books that devote a substantial part of the discussion to ancient speakers. I can't watch them give a PowerPoint presentation, a television interview, or keynote speech! But I can watch Carly.

If you want to spend some time online to watch masterful body language, I would recommend two spokespeople in particular: Carly Fiorina and John Chambers. They use hand gestures with great impact and there's plenty of video of both on the Web.

Here are my notes from the beginning of a Carly Fiorina presentation about a massive new Hewlett Packard product launch in 2003. Notes on hand gestures are in brackets:

> Behind me is a wall representing 158 new consumer products that HP is introducing today [uses left hand to point to the products behind her on stage]. One hundred fifty-eight new products [uses left hand with thumb and forefinger together to emphasize key point]. This is the largest launch in our company's history [raises both hands together].To put it in perspective, we are introducing today almost as many products as there are candidates for the gubernatorial race in California [extends hands apart]! This fall we will spend three hundred million dollars to launch our largest consumer marketing campaign ever—to show you what it means to be at the center of digital experiences [keeps both hands raised above waist and uses left hand to emphasize money spent]. And we're going to start with digital photography... [opens both hands, palms raised upwards].

Fiorina makes effective use of her hands in virtually every sentence. If you watch her presentations, you might also notice she rarely uses a computer clicker to move from slide to slide. She lets someone else do it allowing her to keep both hands free.

John Chambers also uses gestures to great effect. He's a real master and it shows. According to Cisco's Ron Ricci, "John realizes that how his body moves in context to his words has a big impact on his communication." It would be nearly impossible for me to describe how Chambers uses his hands to reinforce his main points. There isn't a sentence in a Chambers presentation in which he isn't actively using his hands to add another dimension to his message, a dimension most speakers fail to achieve. I actually don't think it would even be useful to describe the specific gestures Chambers makes. The point is not to emulate his gestures but to develop your own. But I would urge you to watch Chambers and Fiorina on video, paying particular attention to their body language and hand movements.

Fire on All Cylinders

Brenda Connors studies body language in the world's top leaders. For seventeen years, she served in the state department as the chief of protocol in New York City. In that role, she would coordinate state visits of foreign dignitaries. She's now a research fellow at the Naval War College in Newport, Rhode Island. She agrees that British prime minister Tony Blair is one of the most engaging speakers on the world stage. He's a substantive and complex thinker, says Connors. She can tell through his use of "three-dimensional" gestures. In other words, he uses both hands, frequently above the waist, and he varies his gestures. According to Connors, Blair's gestures are alive and engaging. He uses his body to his greatest potential. "There's no question that he's deeply connected to his message," says Connors. She believes Blair allows himself to feel, and to be free with his gestures. Most presenters keep themselves bound up, with hands directly in front of them or grasping the podium. In contrast, "Blair is wonderfully dynamic and alive," says Connors. "He allows himself to express what's in his heart. He's firing on all cylinders."

Are you firing on all cylinders? Your presentation may have the potential of a twelve-cylinder turbo-charged Roadster but if you're not using your body effectively, it's like running on only four cylinders! Kick up the power of your presentations by using more dynamic body language—pay attention to where you look, how you walk, and what you do with your hands. Great communicators do. Shouldn't you?

Now that you've learned how to exhibit command presence in your presentations, it's time to reveal the ninth Simple Secret.

★ COACHING DRILLS ★

1. **Play the Video.** Visit www.carminegallo.com for video links to great corporate presenters. Pay particular attention to their body language, hand gestures, and posture.

2. **What Do Your Hands Say?** How can you incorporate hand gestures in your next presentation? At what point would gestures make the most sense? Keep your gestures above the waist and stick with what comes naturally.

3. **Pay Attention.** After this chapter, you're likely to pay more attention to hand gestures than you ever have before. That's great. You'll notice that intelligent and charismatic speakers use gestures very frequently. Ask yourself, who uses hand gestures? Who doesn't? Does it make a difference in the power of their presentations? Does it get your attention? Does it win you over?

SIMPLE SECRET #9: WEAR IT WELL

IMAGE IS *ALMOST* EVERYTHING

"Clients love with their hearts, to be sure, but that love starts in their eyes.
Dress like the company you want to become."

HARRY BECKWITH, *WHAT CLIENTS LOVE*

Men's Wearhouse

"Unlocking human potential is what leadership is all about."

MEN'S WEARHOUSE CEO GEORGE ZIMMER

I'm a student of leadership—who has it, who doesn't, and how to get it. You'll recall my story about Matt Eversmann, the Army Ranger who led his troops through a devastating battle in the streets of Mogadishu, Somalia, in 1993. During our conversations for this book, I asked Eversmann for the secret behind his success as a leader. His answer threw me for a moment. But the more I thought about it, the more it made sense.

"It begins with how you wear your uniform," said Eversmann.

The standard for dress in the military is high. Leaders exceed expectations and always look better than their subordinates. For example, when I was a platoon sergeant and my new lieutenants would come in, I reinforced with them that they needed to make sure that their boots were shinier than all their subordinates. A commander should see a soldier's boots and say to himself, "That guy did a great job shining his boots. But they aren't better than mine." It shows your subordinate, who just spent two hours shining his boots, that his boss spent two hours and two minutes working on his boots.

Leaders look better than their subordinates. That answer stuck with me as I continued my research, interviews, and observations to compile the 10 Simple Secrets of the world's greatest business communicators. A few weeks after my talk with Eversmann, I read a book about Ronald Reagan written by a former White House speechwriter. The author made an interesting observation—Reagan always seemed to look better than everyone else—in photographs, staff meetings, and for public appearances (we'll meet Reagan's personal tailor later in the chapter). Eversmann's answer began to make more sense. Leaders always look a little better than their subordinates. And so do the world's greatest business communicators. They look the part—well-dressed, immaculately groomed, and fit to lead.

★ ★ ★

"Clients are flattered when you dress up for the occasion. People are flattered if they feel you consider them important enough to look a little special for them. It's a subtle compliment."
Barbara Corcoran, founder, The Corcoran Group

Communications with a Capital "C"

James Citrin runs the global technology and communications practice for the world's largest private executive search firm, Spencer Stuart. The firm is responsible for 60 percent of *Fortune* 500 CEO placements. Citrin also wrote the business bestseller, *The 5 Patterns of Extraordinary Careers*. Citrin has recruited top CEOs and presidents for companies like Yahoo!, AOL, Intuit, Lucent, MCI, Westin Hotels, and many, many others. He knows what to look for in an executive. More importantly, he knows what modern boards of directors are looking for in today's corporate leaders.

Citrin and I have had long discussions about leadership communications. His insight has been invaluable in crafting the 10 Simple Secrets. "You cannot lead without good communications," says Citrin. But communications, according to Citrin, includes much more than the words you use. Great communicators demonstrating integrity are active listeners and practice what Citrin calls "benevolent leadership"—truly caring for the success of others as you would your own success. That's communications with a capital C!

"How much emphasis do you place on packaging, especially how one looks?" I asked Citrin.

"Nobody would talk about it as important but it's important," Citrin said.

> The proper way it's discussed is, "She has executive presence" or, "He has a 'command.'" But what they are really saying is, do they project neatness? Physically, are they what you expect? Do they dress appropriately to fit the culture? Are they well-groomed? People respond to all these things. There is a bound of acceptable physical presentation. That's not to say that all good decisions happen within bounds, but in terms of getting the nod, the odds are against you if you are outside the bounds.

"If someone you interview for a top position has a commanding presence and dresses well, what does that tell you?" I asked.

"If someone like that walks in to the room, it causes you to relax and mentally check that box," Citrin said. "They look the part. They've passed the first hurdle. Now let's move on." Pass the first hurdle. It's critical to winning 'em over!

★ ★ ★

During a national debate on whether U.S. air marshals should dress down or dress up when they're undercover on an airplane, an official with the Federal Air Marshall Service said, "Professional demeanor, attire, and attitude gain respect. If a guy pulls out a gun and he's got a tattoo on his arm and he's wearing shorts, I'm going to question whether he's a law enforcement officer." Gain respect by dressing appropriately.

The Hidden Camera Doesn't Lie

ABC's John Stossel proved image matters during a feature for the news-magazine *20/20*. Using hidden cameras, millions of viewers got to see what they instinctively knew—attractive people are treated better than less attractive ones. More drivers stopped to help a beautiful woman with car trouble than stopped for a less attractive one. More school kids had a favorable impression of the good looking substitute teacher than the less attractive one. In one segment, the more attractive man was hired for a sales job over the less attractive man with stronger qualifications. And the less attractive man was told there were no open positions! Image isn't everything, but it's close.

Here's the bottom line—we can't all have the movie star looks of Brad Pitt and Charlize Theron, but we can all enhance what we've got with sharp clothes, good grooming, and fitness habits. Let's start by taking a closer look at what's in the closet of the world's greatest business communicators.

★ ★ ★

Two professors from London Guildhall University found a correlation between attractiveness and career success. In a survey of eleven thousand thirty-three-year-olds, the professors found that unattractive men earned 15 percent less than those perceived as attractive. They even equated good looks with a higher probability of lawyers receiving early partnership. I think the proliferation of makeover television shows prove that most of us, with the exception of Cindy Crawford, have room for improvement. More importantly, improving our looks with a better wardrobe, grooming, and exercise could directly translate into more money, more power, and more success.

Trump's Stunning Admission

Great presenters are great dressers. Television business journalist Stuart Varney says, "I dress expensively and well. I wear expensive suits, silk ties, crisp white starched shirts, and highly polished shoes. That's my look." What's your look? All great communicators have one.

Barbara Corcoran told me,

> I decided early on that I would wear bright colors because being
> a woman in a man's world, I wanted to stand apart from the pack.
> I blended in too nicely with the navy blue or gray suits, so I start-
> ed wearing red suits. In a room of five hundred people, they could
> pick me out. I've since gotten away from red. Now I dress in coral,
> orange, strong pinks—very bright colors. It draws the eye and
> holds people's attention.

Corcoran considers her wardrobe carefully. Even when she had nothing she dressed as though she had everything. In her book she writes, "In
business, I believe the best money spent is on things that create the image
of success...perception creates reality. Most people think it's the other
way around."

Great clothes will draw people's attention. And since your listeners will
form their first impressions, and in many cases make up their mind about
you in those first seven seconds, it pays to look your best in any type of
presentation. "The way we dress says a lot about us before we ever say a
word," writes Donald Trump in *How to Get Rich*. Trump used to wear
inexpensive clothes because he didn't think it made a difference. He later
learned that his attitude was "wrong-headed." Trump now buys "very
high-quality shoes, and they seem to last forever, whereas the cheapos
wear out quickly and always looked as cheap as the price I'd paid for them.
The same is true for suits." Is it my imagination or is that the first time
Trump has admitted to being wrong? It would be quite stunning.

Zimmer Guarantees It

While Trump wears expensive Brioni suits (as does Oracle CEO, Larry
Ellison), most corporate presenters can look just as good for a lot less.
George Zimmer is the founder and CEO of the national clothing chain
Men's Wearhouse. His ubiquitous ads have made Zimmer the nation's
most visible suit salesman. Zimmer was twenty-four-years old when he
took $7,000 in savings to start his company. Today Men's Wearhouse is a
$1.3 billion clothing empire. Inspired by another great communicator,
Chrysler's Lee Iacocca, Zimmer became the pitchman for his company in

its advertisements. Zimmer credits his now famous ad lib at the end of a 1985 commercial for giving his company the marketing spark it needed. The tagline he added at the end of that commercial—"I guarantee it"—put his stamp on the company ever since. With seven hundred stores around the country and ten thousand employees, it's safe to say thousands of men are conducting their presentations dressed in ties, shirts, slacks, and suits from Zimmer's company.

Before I interviewed Zimmer, I spent some time in several Men's Wearhouse stores in my local area. I noticed three things. First, every salesperson had nothing but praise for Zimmer, as though they each had a personal relationship with him (I never told anyone that I was writing a book). It tells me Zimmer walks his talk. That's rare in leadership these days but it's good to see. Secondly, I observed that he's promoting suits much more so than during the dot-com boom when "casual Friday" was every day. Thirdly, I was surprised at the low cost of the suits.

I asked Zimmer, "Can you really look good for less than $500?"

"It's no different in apparel than any other item like cars," said Zimmer.

> You can spend a lot less money and still get good quality and look great. At Men's Wearhouse, you can spend $200 to $500. For $500, you get a better suit, but you can spend $200. …The main difference is the cost of the fabric. Fabric represents one-third of the cost of the suit. Often, that's connected to quotas and duties as much as it is to the actual construction of the fabric. It can be more expensive bringing in something from Italy than from Canada because of NAFTA. Again, it's like a car. You can go out and get a heck of a car for $50,000. But you can also get a great car for $15,000.

Zimmer offered wardrobe advice specifically for this chapter. Zimmer says there are three things to keep in mind when buying a suit: Fit, Staples, and Style.

Zimmer's Wardrobe Tips

1. If the Suit Fits, Wear It: "I'm amazed at how ill-fitting suits are on most people," says Zimmer. "A proper-fitting suit is the single most important

aspect of buying a suit, even more important than fabric." Zimmer recommends you bring suits to an expert tailor. The off-the-rack look is out! Was it really in?

2. Staples Hold It Together: "Everyone should have a navy, charcoal (gray), and black suit. You're well covered with these three colors," says Zimmer. It's easy to make these suits look unique with the right accessories like ties, shirts, belts, and shoes.

3. Stay In Style: "I update my closet twice a year because I get a good employee discount," jokes Zimmerman. "But most men should update their wardrobe once a year." This reminds me of a quote I heard on Bravo's *Queer Eye for the Straight Guy:* "Like milk, clothes have an expiration date."

Where Corporate New York Prefers to Shop

Business professionals can find suits from the world's most famous designers at Barneys in Los Angeles and Chicago. But Barneys New York on Madison Avenue is considered the style mecca for businessmen. So when I wanted to find out more about style and spokespeople, where else would I turn? I talked to Tom Kalenderian, Barneys executive vice president and general merchandise manager, about men's fashion, style, and wardrobe.

Kalenderian believes that a business professional who is well-dressed in "better products" as the high-end category is known, will feel better, have higher self esteem, and exude a "sense of comfort and confidence in their presentations." Kalenderian agrees with Zimmer that there is a dramatic trend away from casual clothing and back to the corporate uniform, the suit. But that doesn't mean men can't have their personal style.

"How can men keep up on the latest styles?" I asked Kalenderian.

"You can't do it alone," he said.

Start a relationship with a sales associate in a store who you trust and respect to give you good information. Every major city has a good store. A sales associate will do the job for you based on your needs and preferences. Over the course of a year you'll have someone consistently contacting you with what's new, what's hot, and what's not.

It's not easy keeping up with changes in style. Kalenderian told me that three-button suits became popular in 1998. Today, since they're the norm, people are wearing two-button suits to be different. But unlike the two-button suits of the recent past, the new ones have buttons placed higher on the jacket. Now, how is a corporate spokesperson expected to keep up with that? I sure can't. That's the point. Let someone else keep you up to date.

Here are Kalenderian's Keys for a Knockout Wardrobe:

- You don't have to break the bank for a great suit. You can spend up to $3,000 at Barneys New York. But you don't have to. Prices start at $850. The difference has much to do with the designer, the fabric, and how many hours of craftsmanship [hand-sewing] goes into building the suit. "It's about the level of luxury," says Kalenderian. "You can buy the same model car but order a custom interior. Both are suitable transportation." Sounds a lot like Zimmer. Why are clothing executives fond of the car analogy? I guess it works!
- Don't overwear your clothes. Kalenderian suggests you have at least five suits so you can avoid wearing any one suit twice in a week. He says giving the natural fibers in the suit "a rest" will make them last longer. Hey, we all need a break.
- Avoid too much dry cleaning. Dry cleaning solution, says Kalenderian, "takes the life out of the fabric."
- Finally, don't forget the shoes! Your audience will pay attention to details, especially to the quality of your shoes. "Comfort is key," says Kalenderian. Once you find a designer you like, choose the shoe that's the most comfortable. He suggests the better-made shoes have soles that are stitched instead of cemented. Kalenderian says stitched shoes will only come apart after extraordinary wear and tear.

I Can't Turn You into the President, But I Can Make You Look Like One

George Zimmer may be the most visible suit salesman and Barneys may carry the most visible brands, but George De Paris makes the most visible suits. A Frenchmen who owns a small tailoring shop near the White House, De Paris needs to be close to his clients, who typically live in the White House. For more than forty years, De Paris has been making suits for American presidents, starting with Lyndon Johnson. He's made suits for Ronald Reagan, Bill Clinton, and both Bush Senior and Junior. His clients often call him to the Oval Office to make them suits and ties they can wear for the most visible of occasions, including major speeches like inaugural events and the State of the Union address. I think it's safe to say his suits have seen more television airtime than the top European fashion designers.

A De Paris suit will set you back a minimum of $2,500. But he agrees with Zimmer and Kalenderian; you can find a perfectly good suit for a lot less. It's like ordering a good steak instead of a filet mignon, he says. But the fit is key. "No suit will look good unless it's fitted properly," De Paris told me. "If the store doesn't have expert tailoring, spend the money to get it tailored right."

★ ★ ★

In *Put Your Best Foot Forward,* jury consultant Jo-Ellan Dimitrius writes that in interviews with jurors after trials, they frequently comment about the clothes worn by witnesses and lawyers. "Fit is among the most common observations…Poorly fitting clothing detracts from the impression you make."

The Color of Leadership

De Paris believes the right colors and combination will help a presenter stand out as a leader. So I asked him, "If you could only choose one combination, what would it be? What is the color of leadership?" Here's his recommendation:

Suit: Dark blue (solid or with a fine pinstripe)
Shirt: White or baby blue
Tie: Burgundy

This is the ultimate color combination of leadership, De Paris assures me. And judging by photographs of American presidents in their most important events, it's obvious he's right. These are the colors that look best on television. But more than that, these colors are opposite each other on the color wheel—hues opposite each other on the wheel are considered complimentary. Next time you see a Renaissance painting, pay attention to the color combination. You'll find shades of blue and burgundy. It's the color of leadership. See how it makes you look during your next presentation!

The Perfect Package

As someone who runs the largest job fair for women, Tory Johnson knows what potential employers are looking for in a new hire. Johnson says packaging counts. If a recruiter is evaluating two equal candidates, it would only be human nature for the recruiter to consider the candidate who offers the more "perfect package." According to Johnson, "Not only does that candidate have the right skills and experience, but the one who is put together better will be a better representative for your company. It would be naïve to assume that it doesn't count." Johnson has some wardrobe advice for readers of this book, especially women, who want to pitch, promote, or present themselves in business situations or job interviews:

1. If in doubt about what to wear, stick to the conservative side. "You can never go wrong with basics. It doesn't mean you have to wear a skirt suit. Pants are perfectly acceptable in just about every line of work today. But it would be a pair of business pants or nice slacks over jeans to just about any type of professional event. Avoid clothes that are so obviously tight that someone would make a comment about it or even have a comment in their own mind."

2. Don't go heavy on the makeup or perfume. "A simpler, more natural appearance carries you far. Sometimes less is more. I don't mean that women should avoid makeup or perfume. But avoid excess."

3. Pay attention to details. They count. "No scuffed shoes or missing buttons. Little things like that. Earrings that are too big and flashy for a professional setting. So many times, I will see someone who looks impeccably dressed and they have scuffed shoes and it ruins the look. I hope your professionalism isn't judged on the condition or style of your shoes, but we do live in a society that is obsessed with looks and physical features. So if you have the ability to take two minutes to shine your shoes, it makes sense to go the extra mile."

4. Finally, dress appropriately. "It's important to understand your audience at any given time. If you're going to a casual networking event, you're not going to show up there with high heels and a cocktail dress. You'll want to be appropriate to that setting."

★ ★ ★

In his book *Career Warfare,* John Hancock CEO Dave D'Alessandro told the story of a business presentation he watched by a former Miss America contestant. Even though she had gained forty pounds, she still dressed like she was appearing in a pageant and not a client meeting. The women in the room hated her and the men didn't take her seriously. According to D'Alessandro, "She actually had some substance that was worth listening to, but she made it impossible for people to listen." D'Alessandro says the way you look and the way you dress speaks volumes, more than most people admit. "If you want success at a high level, it's important that you both look the part and act it," writes D'Alessandro.

Don't Serve Turkey for Valentine's Day

Johnson's advice to dress appropriately is very important to consider, but often neglected. Great communicators dress for the culture of their company or industry. Just as I wouldn't expect a spokesman for Tommy Bahama to wear a double-breasted suit and French-cuffed shirts, I wouldn't expect the CEO of an insurance firm to dress in silky Hawaiian shirts. Joe Saul-Sehy, an American Express financial advisor who is part of AE's Centurion Club for public speakers made a great point about dressing appropriately for the culture. He talks to many new financial planners who say they don't want to look like bankers; they want to look different. Joe says there's only one problem with that attitude: your clients expect you to look like a banker!

Joe Saul-Sehy learned about paying attention to details the hard way. Early in his career he did what you expect any good financial planner to do—save money. He decided to save by buying very cheap suits and shoes. One day, he decided to buy shoes that were a little more expensive. When he walked into the office his boss said, "I'm glad you finally got rid of those cheap, plastic shoes." Joe responded, "Why didn't you tell me before?" That's the point. Your listeners, clients, or audience will not tell you that you don't look good. But your clothes speak volumes.

Help for the Wardrobe Challenged

Whether you're a man or a woman, if you think you might be wardrobe-challenged, you'll find some solid advice in a couple of books currently on the market. For women, check out *What Not to Wear* and *What Not to Wear for Every Occasion*. Both books are written by Trinny Woodall and Susannah Constantine. They will teach you more than I can possibly tell you in this chapter, along with great photographs, advice, and examples. I won't pretend I know as much as they do about women's clothes. But Woodall and Constantine show women the best and the worst outfits for virtually every body type and every situation—job interviews, management roles, or a business casual event.

★ ★ ★

Brenda Kinsel has written four books on the subject of women's style and wardrobe including *In the Dressing Room with Brenda*. I've spoken to Kinsel about women's styles because I like her approach—she takes into account a woman's personality, features, and coloring when consulting her clients. As a speaker, Kinsel says, you want your listeners to focus on what she calls your "communication center"—your face. When picking out clothes, Kinsel recommends colors that accent, or "repeat," a woman's natural coloring. For example, "If a woman has sparkling blue eyes, wear a blue blouse that repeats the eye color. It's so pleasant to look at somebody who repeats something

Men who need some help in the closet would do well to read *Chic Simple Dress Smart Men: Wardrobes That Win in the New Workplace* by Kim Johnson Gross and Jeff Stone. The authors describe everything from how to dress for job interviews to what to wear when you're the CEO. They even address the right clothes for presentations: "Without being too ostentatious or visually distracting, the shirt-and-tie combination should reflect power." The advice is followed by colorful photographs of "power combinations."

While these books might be helpful, styles change and do so often. It's hard to keep up. For instance, I always thought wearing a striped tie with a striped shirt was a cardinal sin in men's fashion. One day, I picked up a business magazine and saw an ad for a famous clothing designer. The model in the ad was wearing just such a combination. I started noticing the trend in the top men's stores after that. Hey, why wasn't I copied on the memo? Given the fact that you might have more urgent matters to deal with in your professional life than leafing through magazines or strolling the local mall, here are three secrets to remember from this section:

1. Great communicators dress a little better than everybody else!

2. Great communicators dress well and dress appropriately for the occasion or industry.

3. Great communicators dress to compliment their features, skin tone, and personal brand.

every presentation. Jobs can get away with it. He's a maverick and has built a company with a rebellious reputation. His wardrobe is appropriate for Apple's employees and its customers. It might not be for you. Salesforce.com CEO Marc Benioff has also built a reputation of being a maverick, tackling entrenched competitors with a mix of boldness and brashness. Benioff often wears Hawaiian shirts to work. He loves Hawaii. He has a home there and even named his dog Kona, who, by the way, is a fixture at the office. But most of us should leave the Hawaiian shirts for the company barbecue.

You've Got That Glow!

Nothing compliments a great suit more than radiant, glowing skin. Make no mistake, great communicators take care of their hair and complexion. Stuart Varney says that right before a speech or a presentation, "I will generally take an extremely hot shower and a very close shave. You come out glowing. Your color is good, almost like you're wearing makeup. You come out squeaky clean, you're nailed down—tight, sharp, and crisp. That's my look. That's the look I'm aiming for."

What look are you aiming for? The pasty-white, disheveled look of a mad scientist or the crisp, radiant, and sharp look of the world's most powerful presenters? If it's the latter, then good grooming habits are essential. Listeners notice the details. Hair, nails, skin. People form their impressions on your look. It registers.

You might recognize Kyan Douglas, the grooming guru, from Bravo's hit show, *Queer Eye for the Straight Guy*. He's the first one of the Fab Five to race into someone's bathroom to check out what skin and hair products the typically unkempt straight guy has in his cabinet. Of course, by the end of the show, he and the others have completely made over their subject, usually with amazing results. The Fab Five are everywhere. My wife and I joke that when the dolls hit the shelves, their fifteen minutes of fame are over. But for now, let's take advantage of their advice. In the book, *Queer Eye for the Straight Guy,* Douglas offers his tips for grooming. He suggests that all men should have (and use!) the following products: foaming facial cleanser, moisturizer, exfoliating scrub, shampoo and conditioner, hair products (gel, pomade), razor and shaving cream, nail clippers, deodorant, mouthwash, and nose hair trimmer. You'll look ten—no, one hundred—times better if you use these products before your next presentation! Simple grooming habits will lead to extraordinary results.

Better Than Orgasm? Really?

In the movie *Pumping Iron,* Arnold Schwarzenegger said lifting weights, getting all pumped up, was better than orgasm. While most corporate leaders wouldn't go quite that far, the world's greatest business communicators are strikingly fit. Cisco's John Chambers jogs five miles a day, Sybase CEO John Chen has a gym in his office, and need I say more about Schwarzenegger? In fact, virtually every corporate spokesperson profiled in this book maintains a vigorous exercise schedule. They're fitter than average. And it's critical to their dazzling presentations: they look better, they have better posture, they exude unwavering confidence and optimism, and they have far more energy than everybody in the room.

Brian Halla is the CEO of Silicon Valley's National Semiconductor, one of the largest chip firms in the world. It's a $7 billion company with nearly ten thousand employees. Chances are your cell phone, notebook computer, or flat-screen computer monitor has National's chips inside. Halla is considered one of the great CEOs in corporate America today. He's smart, aggressive, and a confident speaker.

Halla tells me a recent commitment to fitness has made all the difference in his public presentations. During a round of golf, he was huffing and puffing up the eighteenth fairway while a friend looked like he had just teed-off on the first hole. Halla couldn't get through afternoon meetings without feeling tired. Imagine how low energy his presentations must have been by the end of the day.

That's all changed. In September 2002, he and his wife made a commitment to get in shape. They joined a local gym and began working out with a personal trainer. Ten months later, Halla felt like a new person at the age of fifty-six. Halla's doctor says he's lost forty pounds and gained twenty pounds of muscle. Halla, who gives two to three presentations a week, now has "a lot more energy, especially when traveling and giving speeches. I used to run out of breath while speaking. Not anymore. Traveling, especially international travel, used to be like a body slam. Now I can race to the first meeting after stepping off the plane." Halla works out three times a week at 6:30 a.m. with a combination of aerobics and weight training.

★ ★ ★

In a May, 2002, article for *Academy Management Executive,* Ken Cooper, who coined the term aerobics, writes about the executive benefits of fitness and lists top corporate leaders who work out regularly. Among them, Domino's Pizza founder Tom Monaghan. Monaghan "runs about four miles every day or uses a Stairmaster; he uses a Nautilus machine for thirty minutes, alternating upper and lower body every other day; and when traveling does pushups and crunches along with running. He consumes about two thousand calories a day, does not eat any desserts or sweets, and fasts on bread and water for half a day twice a week." Cooper also quotes a study of stock brokers who underwent an intensive twelve-week exercise regime. Those stock brokers who participated in the exercise program earned higher sales commission than those who didn't, all else being equal.

The Terminator Workout

Another chief executive who understands the power of working out is California governor Arnold Schwarzenegger. Schwarzenegger doesn't look like he did when he won seven Mr. Olympia titles. But at fifty-seven, he's in awesome shape. Staffers tell me he works out more than anyone in his office. And he certainly looks the part of a powerful, commanding leader. His schedule running the world's fifth largest economy doesn't offer as much time for training (he used to work out six hours a day while competing in bodybuilding). Regardless, he hasn't abandoned a rather rigorous regime. Schwarzenegger gets up at 6:00 a.m. and begins each day with forty-five minutes on the elliptical trainer in his suite at the Sacramento Hyatt Regency. At the end of each workday in the state capitol, he works out at a local athletic club with weights for another thirty minutes.

That's his training schedule—which is frankly far more exhaustive than most business professionals with a fraction of his responsibilities. The result, as he once told a group of fitness professionals, is that "I never run out of energy." One morning, Schwarzenegger returned to California from a four-day trip to the Middle East. He arrived at 5:00 a.m., in time for a breakfast speech to the California Chamber of Commerce. Journalists and business professionals in the audience were impressed with Schwarzenegger's energy. The governor looked tan, youthful, and as refreshed as ever. It pays to work out!

★ ★ ★

The elliptical training machine is one of the hottest cardio machines on the market today. It can be found at a gym or exercise equipment store near you. It provides a good full-body workout. But other more traditional cardio machines will also do the trick. Researchers at the University of Wisconsin, La Cross, compared the exercise benefits of the elliptical trainer to a treadmill. They found no significant difference in terms of heart rate, oxygen consumption, or calories burned. So whether you prefer an elliptical or treadmill, get on it!

A CEO Trainer for CEOs

Speakers who work out regularly look the part. They have more energy, better posture, and exude more confidence than most others who don't exercise. Scott Norton, the founder and CEO of Axis Performance Center in Menlo Park, California, isn't surprised. Norton blew out his knee during his first year of playing football for the University of Utah. Turning a setback into an opportunity, Norton spent the next three years as a strength coach. After graduating, Norton spent another five years as a personal trainer before opening up his own center that caters to top executives in the San Francisco Bay area. In true Silicon Valley fashion, a venture capitalist even provided Norton the capital for him to open his facility! He opened Axis in 1996 and now has more than one thousand clients who work with fifty-five trainers—the best trainers Norton could recruit from around the world.

I spoke to Norton as we stood on the training floor of the Menlo Park facility, surrounded by a flurry of sweat and activity and bodies in motion—the clanging of weights behind us, the whirring of treadmills to our left, a trainer pushing his client to perform "two more reps" to our right. Some of his clients, among the wealthiest and most powerful executives in the San Francisco Bay area, hit the gym by 6:00 a.m. for workouts that last one to one and a half hours.

★ ★ ★

Exercise sends oxygen-rich blood to the brain. People who exercise are shown to do better on tests requiring critical thinking. If regular aerobic exercise can make you think better, then it should make you speak better. Exercise will help you think and speak more clearly, with more focus and with more energy.

"Why do these busy professionals carve out so much time to work out?" I asked Norton.

"Carmine, they have no choice. Fitness is part of the plan for the way they're going to live their life. They have to prepare their bodies to handle the demands of everyday life. They get up at six and work until midnight sometimes. They fly around the world, five or six countries in a week. They travel and they work. They can't afford not to workout. If they don't train, they will not have the strength, endurance, and ability to think on their feet."

Norton continues, "They're communicating and presenting all day—talking to clients, customers, employees, vendors—it's never ending. Their bodies have to be able to handle it. They need strength, control, and flexibility."

"When it comes to speaking and presenting, can you see a big difference between those CEOs committed to fitness and those who are not?" I asked Norton.

Absolutely. I see enthusiasm, passion, eye contact, posture, and confidence. With these individuals, life doesn't get easier. It's important they prepare their bodies to handle it. Over the years, the body breaks down. After the age of twenty-five, your body will lose about five pounds of muscle every ten years. But if you do strength training, you don't lose it, you increase it—the bones, ligaments, and muscles all benefit. You'll have better posture. Better posture makes you look and feel more confident, you'll smile more and radiate leadership. Executives train to perform at their highest level. Without it, you'll look and sound like a dud during interviews, presentations, or board of director meetings. The executive who trains regularly will look and feel energized. He's passionate. He radiates energy. He makes his listeners feel alive!

★ ★ ★

One word about cosmetic surgery—it seems to be all the rage these days with shows like *Extreme Makeover*. And it's certainly not just for women anymore. Men are getting face-lifts, tummy-tucks, and all other sorts of tucks, pulls, and lifts. You need to make up your own mind on whether or not such procedures are for you, but please consider it carefully. Rigorous exercise and a healthy diet has proven to dramatically slow the effects of aging. Try it first. In the February 9, 2004, issue of *Fortune,* human resources consultant David Carpe was quoted as saying, "Forget about the superficial stuff like cosmetic surgery and dyeing your hair. You'll just look desperate." Instead, he urged older job seekers to exercise, eat right, and get enough sleep. "I see people in their seventies who are vibrant, energetic, and in great demand," Carpe said.

"Look as great as you are," writes Harry Beckwith in *Selling the Invisible*. Great communicators look like the great speakers that they are. They dress well, they're well-groomed, and they're in great shape. Do the same. Remember, you're competing against them.

Now that we've covered the basics of packaging the spokesperson, it's time to reveal the tenth Simple Secret.

The Ultimate Presentation & Fitness Diet

Diet, exercise, and fitness are so important to maintaining vitality and energy as a presenter, I spoke to personal trainer, Scott Norton, about recommendations we could offer business professionals who need to perform their best. With Norton's permission, here are the nutritional recommendations offered clients at the Axis Performance Center:

The basics

Eat several small meals a day

This will stabilize your energy levels and keep your metabolism active.

Balance your meals

A blend of carbohydrates (45-60%), proteins (15-25%), and fats (15-30%) are essential. Find what combination works best for you.

Eat fruits and vegetables

Eat as much as you can—organic is best! At least one serving each meal is ideal to consume the vitamins, minerals, and fiber your body needs for optimum health.

Fat is good!

Avoid the trans-fats (partially hydrogenated) and saturated fats, but consume fish oils and flax-seed oils and other foods containing Omega-3 and -6 fatty acids which are essential for your body's chemistry.

Drink lots of water!

Eight glasses per day or half your body weight in ounces per day are two guidelines to follow. Increase your intake if you exercise or consume caffeine.

Take a multivitamin

Even if you eat well, you may need a supplement—consult a health or nutrition specialist for more specific considerations.

Weight loss

Avoid big meals at dinner and late-night snacking.

Your metabolism slows as evening approaches so you don't need to consume as many calories.

Plan meals in advance

This enables you to control the balance between carbs, protein, and fats, and how much you eat.

Slow down when you eat and enjoy your food

The slower you eat, the more time your body has to recognize that you are full.

Be aware of portion sizes

Restaurant portions are too large.

Don't skip meals!

If you skip meals, your body thinks that you are starving it and will go into conservation mode. Hence your body will store the calories instead of burning them as fat.

Performance

Fuel one to three hours before exercise (or a major presentation). This will prevent you from getting prematurely fatigued by ensuring that your glucose stores are fully stocked.

Replenish within one hour post-exercise with a balanced meal

Recovery is key, and it starts with carbohydrates to replenish your glucose stores, protein for muscle recovery, and fat for cell recuperation.

Increase overall caloric intake to recover and build muscle

Intense training takes a lot of energy, so make sure you are getting enough overall calories to sustain energy levels and rebuild muscle.

Replenish electrolytes

When electrolytes are depleted, it can lead to decreased function or muscle cramping. Because electrolytes are lost in sweat, they need to be replenished during and after your workouts (Gatorade or bananas work well).

Good foods

Good fat (sources of Omega-3 fats)

Cold-water fish (salmon, shark)

Avocado

Nuts (all natural nut butters)

Olive oil, flax-seed oil (unheated)

Sunflower seeds

Higher-fiber carbohydrates

Vegetables (dark greens, corn, peas)

Fruits (apple, kiwi, pear, strawberries)

Oats

Whole wheat products

Whole grain, low sugar cereals

Healthy protein sources

Nuts

Lean red meats

Skinless chicken and turkey

Eggs

Fish

Legumes

Pitfalls

Beware of fad diets.

Minimize intake of caffeine, alcohol, and soda.

Avoid processed foods and trans fats (partially hydrogenated oil).

Avoid energy bars as a regular meal replacement.

PART FOUR

LEAVE 'EM WANTING MORE

Now that you've learned how to talk, walk, and look like a leader, it's time to reveal the last Simple Secret that will make your transformation complete. In this last part, you'll hear from business professionals who are compelling to listen to because they continue to be relevant to twenty-first-century audiences. People want to hear from them because they know they'll learn something new. Everyone wants to leave your talk having learned something they didn't know before.

In this section, you'll learn:

- How to captivate your audience every time and leave them wanting more by keeping your message current
- How great corporate speakers continue to transform themselves with every presentation and excel at communicating change
- How to keep the power in your PowerPoint presentations
- The single greatest secret to take away from this book

It's time to reveal the Simple Secret that will make your transformation complete. Are you ready? Let's go!

SIMPLE SECRET #10: REINVENT YOURSELF

MADONNA OR ROCKY. IT'S YOUR CHOICE.

"You only get one shot. Do not miss your chance to blow."

EMINEM

Richard Lewin 2004

One thousand Elvis imperson-ators roam the corridors and showrooms of Las Vegas hotels, but only one can claim the title of Entertainer of the Year. It's Danny Gans, the singer and impressionist who landed a ten-year, $100 mil-lion contract to play at the Mirage in his own theatre. There's one big difference between Gans and thousands of other wanna-bes: Gans reinvents himself in every show. Yes, he can be Elvis. Yes, he can do the old favorites like Frank

"The material needs to be well written, concise, and compelling. But it also needs to be presented in an interesting manner. Don't ignore either."

VENTURE CAPITALIST AND BROADWAY
COMIC DAVID MOORE

Sinatra, Dean Martin, Sammy Davis, and the rest of the Rat Pack. But he can also be Michael Bolton, Al Pacino, Dr. Ruth, and Creed. In fact, audi-ences don't know quite what to expect because Gans himself doesn't know before the show. He has the ability to customize each appearance based on his audience that night, their reaction to the first few minutes of the show and what's happening in the news that day. No two shows are ever the same.

In *Showbiz Magazine,* Hilary Green writes, "He [Gans] gauges the audience's taste and customizes each performance to fit their collective taste. At one moment, Gans may move flawlessly from an on-the-money David Bowie or Eric Clapton to Janet Jackson or Kenny Loggins without missing a beat. Gans interjects topical subjects into his show, too, often including an event that may have occurred that day. Sometimes members of the audience will shout out requests, which prompts Gans to come up with a new character on the spot. You never know who'll show up on the stage!"

Great entertainers stay fresh and remain contemporary if they hope to appeal to new audiences. The queen of reinvention, Madonna, even named her 2004 world tour Reinvention. The longest running show in theatre history, *Beach Blanket Babylon,* reinvents itself every few months, literally. Its musical parodies are based on pop culture so the show updates its spoofs and adds new characters and songs throughout the year. Thirty years after *Beach Blanket Babylon* started in San Francisco, it still plays to packed houses around the world. Great business communicators take a cue from great entertainers: they infuse their presentation with fresh stories, they constantly seek to improve their speaking skills, and they always seek to incorporate the latest strategies, ideas, and cultural references into their presentations, speeches, or meetings.

Think back to a favorite teacher in high school or college. What made him or her stand out? A sincere interest in his or her students? That's part of it. But I always preferred instructors who peppered their lessons with references that were relevant to my life. It made a huge difference in how much I enjoyed their classes. Remember the key question every audience member is asking him or herself—why do I care? It's easier to answer that question by being contemporary.

★ ★ ★

The world's top coaches are also evolving with new technologies, using the latest gadgets and software to boost their team's performance. San Jose Sharks head coach Ron Wilson is a self-described "techno-geek." In his first full season, he took the hockey team from the bottom of their division to the Stanley Cup semi-final. Wilson uses a tablet PC hooked up to a digital video recorder to instantly mark, review, and analyze plays. He shows players how to exploit weaknesses in the opponents defense by marking up the screen on the video as well. As one coach put it, "Would you give a presentation to IBM or Microsoft on a chalkboard?"

Rocky VI? Say It Isn't So!

Don't get me wrong. I like Sylvester Stallone. He has a lot of admirable qualities. But knowing when to hang up the gloves isn't one of them. As I'm writing this, I hear he's working on *Rocky VI*. I hope the rumor isn't true. I didn't even know there was a *Rocky V*! Seriously.

Unlike the *Rocky* franchise, great business communicators stay fresh. They fill their presentations with topical references because they keep up on popular culture, current events, or the latest management books and strategies. Klaus Kleinfeld is the CEO of the U.S. division of Siemens, the $86 billion industrial giant. Ask him about popular music and he can go on about the latest hip-hop star and the artist's contribution to the music scene. As a doctorate and MBA, Kleinfeld is equally at ease discussing the latest strategic management theories. In a profile for *USA Today*, a senior vice president for marketing at Siemens said, "I worked at GE with Jack Welch, and I worked in the Reagan administration. I've never met a person who is as good a communicator as Klaus. It's a combination of his tremendous curiosity and his energy."

★ ★ ★

Virgin's Richard Branson reinvents himself by constantly looking for new opportunities and adventures. The Virgin Group is now involved in planes, trains, finance, soft drinks, music, mobile phones, holidays, cars, publishing, bridal wear—you name it—all tied together by Branson's insatiable curiosity. In *Losing My Virginity*, Branson writes, "By nature I am curious about life, and this extends to my business. That curiosity has led me down many unexpected paths and introduced me to many extraordinary people." Be curious. Learn something new and transmit that information to your audiences. You'll stand out.

Curiosity is the key word. Kleinfeld's curiosity keeps him fresh and contemporary—exactly what twenty-first-century audiences crave. In fact, most, if not all, of the great communicators profiled in this book are remarkably current. Here's what some of them have to say about this topic.

Suze Orman: "I never use the same story twice. Money is fluid. If I use a story, it happened a few minutes before I speak or it comes up spontaneously. When one has a stable of stories, it takes you back to the past rather than keeping you in the moment where you need to be. I try to keep my mind clear and have the faith that when I need something it will be there. Otherwise, I have to think back to a story. It takes me out of the moment. If I lose my audience for one second, I've lost them. I never, ever use the same story twice."

Martin Gagen, Former executive director, 3i Venture Capital: "Always make it current. In every presentation, I include something that happened today. I use it as a bridge to a point I'm trying to make. For example, I had to give a presentation on the day ex-Beatle George Harrison passed away. My speech was all about achievement; are we creating a legacy? So I started by talking about George Harrison, his music, his life, and the fact that he has left a legacy. I encouraged the audience to think about the legacy they want to leave. I used it as a bridge to my topic."

Jeff Taylor, Founder, Monster: "Many executives don't get out much. They understand their company or product but have no idea how it actually applies to the world. Become an expert in your industry as well as your company or product. You have to be willing to change. A lot of people get known for one thing in their life. Like Henry Winkler getting stuck with Fonzi and never getting out of that character. Or Gary Coleman or William Shatner. Within your business, it's important to change and evolve, like Madonna."

David Moore, Venture capitalist and stand-up comic: "There is no better exercise for communicating than doing stand-up comedy. Imagine giving a presentation to a group of employees, and having them rate each one of your 'points' by either clapping—or staring blankly. Performing stand-up has helped me learn the importance of concise language, getting to the point quickly, trimming unnecessary sentences, and, most importantly, to keep it interesting (and funny!). Since I am constantly working on new material, I think my language, writing, and speaking skills have never been better."

Howard Schultz, Chairman, Starbucks: "Companies that embrace the status quo and do not push for reinvention or self-renewal will find themselves in deep trouble. I think great leaders continue to run, take in new information, are willing to make mistakes, and refine their style."

★ ★ ★

In *Pour Your Heart into It,* Howard Schultz writes about hiring Scott Bedbury as head of marketing because he brought new, innovative, and exciting ideas that would help Starbucks stay fresh as their customers' likes and interests evolved. According to Schultz, "Scott believes that Starbucks should be a 'knowing' company: in on the latest jokes, the latest music, the latest personalities, up to date about politics, literature, sports, and cultural trends." In other words, Bedbury would continue to reinvent the company to meet the demands of contemporary society. Every company needs someone like Bedbury. And every spokesperson should adopt his attitude.

Extreme Communication Makeovers

Reinvention involves a lot more than staying current. It's about making a commitment to improvement. There's no such thing as a natural-born presenter. There are naturally gregarious, outgoing people who find it easier to adopt winning presentation techniques, but they weren't born as gifted speakers. Stick with me on this and I'll prove it. The world's greatest business communicators evolve, often through trial, error, and failures. Many have had to overcome challenges most of us never have to face. But they were determined to master communication skills because they realize their personal success and the success of their companies depend on their ability to win over their audiences.

If You Don't Have Big Breasts, Put Ribbons on Your Pigtails

I love the title of Barbara Corcoran's book, *If You Don't Have Big Breasts, Put Ribbons on Your Pigtails.* The title of her first book, *Use What You've Got,* was the politically correct title for the book's first edition. Her publisher insisted on it. But once the book became a hit, the publisher agreed to her original title idea for the paperback edition. Same book. Different title. It's funny how authors tend to have more clout when their books become *New York Times* bestsellers!

Corcoran was building her New York real estate empire when she had a terrifying speaking experience. Citibank had invited Corcoran to speak at their first annual "Seminar for Home Buyers." Corcoran thought it would be a good way to generate some free advertising. It was her first public speech and she took the time to prepare for it—reviewing the content, rewriting drafts, and practicing. When she was introduced to eight hundred people in the audience, Corcoran strolled up to the podium and started with what she had been taught in the public-speaking books: a joke. Bad move. She forgot the punch line and couldn't find the index card on which she wrote it! Everything unraveled from there. She couldn't speak, literally. She opened her mouth and nothing came out. She slumped back to her seat while the shocked moderator introduced the next speaker. To say she was mortified would be an understatement. She thought she would never speak in front of a group again.

That's the way Corcoran related the story to me when we spoke. But as a corporate communicator who was determined to reinvent herself, her story has a good ending. Most speakers would hide from the public for the rest of their careers after an incident like that. Not Corcoran. That's not how she turned a $1,000 loan into a billion-dollar empire. She saw an opportunity to improve on this aspect of her life, and did so.

The very next day she called NYU and pitched a course on real estate sales. Corcoran even claimed she was an "excellent speaker"! She taught courses at the university for the next five years and really did become the excellent public speaker that she originally claimed. Another benefit—in Corcoran's first class, she met a young dynamo named Carrie Chang. Chang not only joined Corcoran's group, she became New York's condominium queen, selling more condos than anyone. When Chang started, condo sales accounted for 5 percent of real estate sales in New York. By 2002, condos accounted for more than 35 percent of city sales. Corcoran rode the wave and would have completely missed it had it not been for meeting Chang after her public speaking debacle.

As Corcoran told me, "I was rewarded for not being a good communicator!" Corcoran took what could be perceived as a negative experience and turned it into something empowering. How many people would have completely abandoned any hope of becoming a great corporate speaker after an experience like Corcoran's? Would you have bounced back? Successful speakers use setbacks as stepping stones.

★ ★ ★

The Great Communicator wasn't always a great communicator. It took work. When President Ronald Reagan passed away on June 5, 2004, *Time* magazine devoted a special issue to America's fortieth president. Reporter Nancy Gibbs wrote that it was only after Reagan's acting career began to draw to a close that he developed the speaking skills we're familiar with. In the 1950s, General Electric hired Reagan to host a weekly television show and to give speeches around the country on behalf of the company. It was during that time, Gibbs writes, that Reagan polished his delivery: "Reagan once figured that in his 8 years at GE, he had visited every one of the company's 139 plants, met more than 250,000 employees, spent 4,000 hours talking to them and 'enjoyed every whizzing minute of it.'"

Reagan really did have the 10 Simple Secrets down cold. After his death, columnists wrote about his powerful personality and magnetic speaking skills. One newspaper quoted D. Joel Wiggins from the *Encyclopedia of Television:* "He [Reagan] captured the audience's attention by appealing to shared values, creating a vision of a better future, telling stories of heroes, evoking memories of a mythic past, exuding a spirit of 'can-do' optimism, and converting complex issues into simple language the people could understand and enjoy." How many Simple Secrets did you count?

"I'll Be Back...As a Master Presenter!"

Arnold Schwarzenegger spoke little English when he first arrived in America. A studio actually hired an actor to voice-over Schwarzenegger's voice in the movie *Hercules in New York*. Schwarzenegger attacked his language barrier with the same razor-like focus and determination he brings to everything else in his life. Schwarzenegger's close friend and advisor Paul Wachter tells me that Schwarzenegger was a natural ad-libber, but not a natural presenter. He had to work at it. Schwarzenegger approached the task as a great athlete. Just as Michael Jordan practiced harder than most of his peers to dominate basketball and just as Jerry Rice was the hardest working man in football, Schwarzenegger approached public speaking as his next goal to conquer.

According to Wachter, the tide turned when Schwarzenegger founded the Inner City Games in 1995. That launched his charity work in a big way. It also launched his practice as a speaker. "He started giving more speeches," says Wachter.

"I, along with others, would look to find him speaking opportunities. Arnold is so focused that reporters would say he was 'practicing' to be governor, but he was simply trying to practice speaking. He knew, in one way or another, that the next phase of his life would require that he be out there—more visible. He didn't quite know what he would do next—more charity work, direct movies, or run for office. But he knew whatever he did would require more public speaking. Giving as many speeches as he could was a fun way to improve. That's Arnold. He's always determined to sharpen his skills. Presentations are no exception." Do you seek out every opportunity to practice your presentations?

"Practice, practice, practice. Most nervous speakers try to make as few speeches as possible. The result is they never improve. Practice your speaking skills in non-threatening situations. Volunteer to give the short welcome speech to new members of your church or synagogue. Volunteer to speak to new parents at your child's school. Chair a committee for a local charity and give the monthly report at a board meeting. Another great way to practice is to teach a class. Teachers have to stand up and speak in front of a group every week. One semester of teaching and you will be much more comfortable in front of an audience."
Pat Dean, Annenberg School of Journalism, UCS

Dyslexia Didn't Keep Him Down

Cisco's John Chambers once made a startling admission at a parents' day for his daughter's school. A girl in the audience stumbled as she asked him a question and became embarrassed over her dyslexia. "That's okay," said Chambers. "Take your time. I'm disabled too."

Hard work and a lot of tutoring helped Chambers overcome his dyslexia. But to this day, he despises long memos and rehearses everything he's going to say before a presentation. Chambers continues to evolve as a presenter. According to senior Cisco executives, Chambers has become less dependent on slides and more in tune with his audience. Chambers didn't always stroll through the audience during his presentations. That "Baptist-minister" quality has evolved as he strived to improve his delivery of the Cisco message.

Chambers, Corcoran, and Schwarzenegger are far from being the only ones to overcome serious setbacks but they all share these simple secrets to jump their hurdles: they are committed to improving their presentation skills, they put themselves out there, and they solicit feedback.

Start noticing the speakers around you. You're surrounded by awesome presenters: on television, on radio, in your company, at a conference. Great corporate spokespeople are everywhere. Ask yourself who wins over their audience and why. The best presenters will stand out. You'll begin your growth as a presenter simply by identifying their simple secrets. I became a much better television journalist by watching the great television news stars of our time and working side by side with them. I've become a better presenter after talking to speakers in this book and incorporating some of their techniques in my own professional communications. We all have room to improve.

You Can't Critique Yourself

You've heard the adage, "You are your toughest critic." That's true for some of us. The rest suffer from *American Idol* Syndrome, a particularly harmful affliction that can strike anyone at any age, causing people to think they're much better than they are at singing, speaking, or virtually any endeavor they attempt. Each of the speakers mentioned above are immune to this debilitating syndrome because they actively seek out feedback—honest, critical, and open. Not only did Barbara Corcoran teach a class to improve her public speaking ability, she asked me questions about what I had learned in my research since she was close to signing a deal for a national television network. Schwarzenegger has a small group of trusted friends and advisors who help him prepare speeches and presentations. John Chambers relies on Ron Ricci and his marketing team for honest and critical feedback. Chambers has even had formal communications coaching, as have most of the world's top executives.

Ditch Paula

Wherever you decide to look for feedback—friends, colleagues, coaches—find a Simon Cowell to balance out a Paula Abdul. Have I lost you? Simon Cowell and Paula Abdul are judges on the hit Fox show, *American Idol*. Cowell is caustic, tough, and straight-talking; Abdul softens the blow. Cowell will say, "You are the worst singer I've ever heard"; Abdul will say, "You had pitch problems. That wasn't your best. But I admire you for trying."

Executive presenters need a Cowell in their lives. You see, if you're dull, boring, and uninspiring, nobody in your office will tell you. Not your friends, your colleagues, and certainly not your employees. Most of the time, neither will your boss. I've had bosses tell me all sorts of things about the VPs and directors who will be attending my seminar. Remember the boss who said he wanted me to help transform a particular salesman because he "looked like a beaten dog, no confidence, no energy, no spark"? Well, in less than two hours we had turned that beaten dog into a Doberman with confidence, energy, and sizzle. And that's the point. I can be Cowell when I need to—a no-holds-barred, in-your-face kind of guy. Executives who attend my seminars know what they're getting. Sure, I'm diplomatic and focus on a person's strengths, even build on those strengths, but the only way a presenter can go from dull to dazzling in as short a time as two hours is by hearing open, honest, and critical feedback.

This get-tough approach goes against the instruction at some large public speaking organizations. Joe Saul-Sehy from American Express once started a speaking club for financial advisors in his Michigan town. He said the problem was that nobody wanted to hurt the other person's feelings. "Nobody would say you're slouching, you're rambling, what are you thinking?" Often it's the lack of this type of honest criticism that fuels an inflated self-opinion. Get honest and candid feedback on your presentation style. You can't afford not to.

★ ★ ★

Joe Saul-Sehy makes the most of his public speaking skills. He so impressed producers at a Detroit television station they gave him his own segment. He is now the Friday Money Man. Saul-Sehy is an up-and-comer in American Express and can legitimately claim that the vast majority of his clients, 155 out of 170, are a direct result of his public presentations, on television or in front of local groups. Saul-Sehy had to reinvent himself as well. He stuttered so badly that growing up kids called him "jackhammer." They're not laughing anymore.

Communicating Change

Few presentations are more important in the life cycle of a company, product, service, or cause than during times of change. It's precisely during these times of flux when great leaders undergo a major reinvention, transforming themselves into a calm, reassuring, and confident presence. Unfortunately, this is where most corporate leaders fall short and why most employees are disillusioned with their superiors.

I seriously began to think about leadership and communications early in my television career when I worked as an anchor for a Fox affiliate in California. As you might recall, the economy went through a severe downturn in the early '90s. California was especially hard hit with a huge loss in technology, manufacturing, and military-defense jobs. The advertising slump decimated local television advertising budgets.

One day, the television station I worked at called a company-wide meeting. You know the type—the dreaded "unscheduled" company meeting. The owner flew in from Seattle on his corporate jet and made a brief announcement—the station's GM had been fired, the station wasn't doing well, and there would be layoffs. That's it. That's all he said. His announcement lasted all of one minute. Everyone sat there stunned. Finally, someone asked a question, "How many people will lose their jobs?" The owner answered, "Take a look around. It's safe to say that the person next to you won't be there tomorrow." With that, he walked out, boarded his jet, and flew home. I survived that round of layoffs and continued a long stint as the station's main anchor before leaving for a job with Lou Dobbs at CNN. But to this day, I'll never forget the single worst example of communicating change I had ever seen.

★ ★ ★

During the time I spent writing this book, I would occasionally visit a coffee shop in the nearby downtown. It meant I had to stray from Starbucks every now and then but this downtown shop had big tables, free Internet access, and I could walk to it. I did notice the people who worked behind the counter were not nearly as well-trained, knowledgeable, or engaging as Starbucks employees. One morning I went to the coffee shop expecting to get a lot of work done on a particular chapter and wouldn't you know it, a sign on the door said "OUT OF BUSINESS." I later learned that the owners, who rarely communicated to the employees, announced that they would close this particular shop to spend money expanding another location. The employees learned about it in the middle of the afternoon and were on the street a few minutes later, as were customers in the shop at the time! If I had to bet on it, I would tell you the new and expanded coffee shop probably won't last a year.

Communication starts at the top. If salespeople or employees fail to do a good job communicating to customers, it's a sure sign those at the top fail to communicate to their subordinates. Doesn't communication make good business sense? Why is this a difficult concept for most leaders to understand? Walk into a Starbucks and you'll find knowledgeable, articulate, and enthusiastic staff. It starts from the top. Walk into a Men's Wearhouse and you'll find the same. It starts from the top. Howard Schultz once wrote, "Starbucks can't flourish without the passionate devotion of our employees." I can see why. The ability to communicate clearly, concisely, and accurately is the first criteria required to be a new manager at Starbucks. If you're at the top, or if you want to get there, make sure great communication starts with you.

One-Hundred-Year Flood

Fast forward ten years from my experience at that local television station. California faced another downturn, this time even more severe than the early '90s. The dot-com bubble had burst, taking the stock market down with it along with more than $7 trillion of wealth. Suddenly, Cisco Systems, whose equipment makes the Internet function, saw a steep decline in orders. John Chambers had no choice but to lay off some six thousand employees—the biggest workforce reduction in the company's history. Chambers was emotionally devastated. But instead of cowering, Chambers expressed his deep disappointment at the turn of events and encouraged open and honest communication with the remaining employees. He didn't end his monthly breakfast meetings with employees to celebrate birthdays and encouraged tough questions from everybody. He shared a vision for where the company was heading.

According to corporate positioning VP Ron Ricci, Chambers also insisted on giving out one of the most generous severance packages Silicon Valley had ever seen. Cisco has since weathered the storm, the "one-hundred-year flood" as Chambers likes to say, enjoys the lowest turnover of employees in its category, and just recently was voted one of the best companies to work for by *Fortune* magazine. Oh, and they're hiring thousands of people once again. The amazing part of this story is that I spoke to people who had been laid off and not one of them had a bad word to say about Chambers. That's the kind of reputation only built by a communicator who lives the 10 Simple Secrets and champions change!

Turning Around a 150-Year-Old Institution

During the writing of this book, Reuters, the legendary news service company, was going through some of the biggest changes of its 150-year history. As he mentioned earlier, President Devin Wenig had the task of communicating to the company's employees why Reuters was paring down its product offerings from one thousand three hundred to thirty-five. That's a tough message to communicate to some nineteen thousand employees and salespeople. Wenig articulated the changes masterfully.

"This is a deep change for a company that wasn't used to being changed," Wenig told me.

I think that in periods like this, the first principle is to communicate often. It's vital. It's easier to change a strategy, a product set, etc. The hardest thing to change is a culture, what people feel in their hearts and minds. You must touch people often with clear messages about where the organization is going and why it's heading there, especially in times that are unsettling. Like when you're communicating to people whose friends have been laid off or to people working on products we say we are no longer going to sell. Human beings by nature are unsettled by change. Communicating often and clearly about why we're getting through this, how we're doing this, and where we're going to end up is so vital in times of change.

Communicate often. It's essential to winning over your customers and employees.

Quick follow-up: Wenig wrote me in the summer of 2004 to say the turnaround was "going great." The company's stock had rebounded four-fold, revenue and profits were growing, and "there are positive signs of revitalization in our culture." Wenig won't say it, but I will—he's partly responsible for the improvement in the firm's morale. It's the kind of spirit only a great communicator can impart on his or her organization. It reminds me of John Hancock CEO Dave D'Alessandro, who said you should strive to be the kind of coach people want to play for. In *Career Warfare* D'Alessandro writes, "The difference between what can be accomplished by a group of people who are willing to do only the minimum and a group of people who are willing to go the extra mile for you is enormous."

★ ★ ★

"The most important thing a CEO can do is to communicate his values every day," says Starbucks chairman Howard Schultz. Great leaders of service companies live this principle. Every day at every one of the Ritz Carlton's fifty-seven hotels, fifteen minutes are set aside to discuss the company's core values with the hotel chain's fifty-seven thousand employees.

A Monster Reinvention, and Another, and Another

"Chief Monster" Jeff Taylor always seeks to reinvent himself and the company he founded, Monster—today the biggest online job-search website with revenues of nearly half a billion a year. Taylor isn't content to sit behind a computer in his office every day. He gives up to seventy speeches a year and, on occasion, can be found spinning albums as a DJ at Boston's The Palace.

"Be willing to change," says Taylor. "But communicate those changes consistently," he adds. In its ten-year history, Monster has continued to reinvent its slogan, or tagline, to reflect changes in what job seekers and employers seem to care about at a particular time. The taglines are meant to resonate with ever-changing career environments. Monster has changed its slogan no fewer than four times in the last decade, beginning with "There's a better job out there." Other slogans include "Never Settle," "Declare Your Independence," and "Today's the Day."

Regardless of the slogan, the message is communicated consistently in all of Monster's marketing material and advertising: in print, on radio, on the Internet, and in Taylor's presentation. Taylor keeps his brand fresh by reinventing it virtually every two years, but his presentations evolve as well.

★ ★ ★

"The difference between great and average or lousy in any job is, mostly, having the imagination and zeal to re-create yourself daily."
Tom Peters, *The Pursuit of Wow!*

We Have a PowerPoint Problem

There are more than forty million PowerPoint (PPT) presentations given daily. As you probably know, PPT is Microsoft's powerful presentation software program. If you don't know, then I'm glad you made it to the last chapter. Learning PPT and how to interact with the program is critical to reinventing yourself as a presenter. Did you know they're using PPT as early as elementary school? Teachers and kids are using it! If a seventh grader can reinvent with it, so can you.

I'm not talking about simply learning how to create a slide. Any good book on PPT can teach you that in five minutes. No, I'm talking about really interacting with PPT so it compliments and enhances your presentation.

It's safe to say most PPT presentations are awful. Ask anyone who has to watch presentations for a living, like venture capitalists. They'll back me up on this. The VCs I talk to acknowledge the vast majority of presentations are terrible. Among the biggest problems:

Too many slides: Sybase CEO John Chen told me he uses a total of twelve slides for a one-hour presentation. "Most people would double that number," Chen said. "But you will lose your audience if you overdose on information. The bigger the audience, the more concise you must be. With larger audiences, throw out the 'rule of three' and focus on one central theme. For smaller groups, you can develop sub-themes but no more than three or four." Remember when I told you about the client with fifty-two PPT slides for a one hour presentation? Nobody wants to see that many slides, no matter how much you worked on them.

I asked Sybase CEO John Chen how much emphasis he places on communication skills when hiring new executives. "Very, very important," he said. "We assume engineers, salespeople, and managers have the basic training and experience. But do they have the right attitude? Are they concise, passionate? Do they have the ability to answer questions clearly? Are they willing to communicate? Some people are brilliant but they don't want to communicate, they just don't want to. I respect that. But they will never be a CEO."

Too many words and numbers: Television news and MTV-style videos have turned us into a very visual society. Too much text and too many numbers are a sure and fast way to bore your audience. They'll be looking at their watches in the first two minutes of your talk. This is the dreaded data-dump. It's to be avoided.

Jeff Taylor tries to avoid more than seven words on a slide. That's pretty impressive. "We have a PPT problem," Taylor told me.

Our entire business world is falling into a trap. Every meeting has a slide show and every slide has a headline and four or five bullets. Sometimes, you have a chart and three bullets. We go from meeting to meeting and slide to slide. We are losing our ability to be creative and to creatively express ideas and concepts. As a leader, move out of the comfort zone of a straight, squared up PPT presentation. When I present, my presentations tend to have a billboard strategy: Use seven words or less or don't bother. That means you actually have to know the topic. Most people read the headline and the bullets. It's the idea you want to get across. For example, one slide could outline our strategy: "Fish where the fish are." I can speak for fifteen minutes to five hundred people with only those words on the slide.

By the way, Taylor only uses eleven slides in a one-hour presentation and doesn't even get to his first slide until he's been speaking for fifteen minutes. That's engaging!

Let's be honest. Taylor's "billboard" strategy of seven words or less is fine for some slides, but there are times when you need to deliver a bit more information. You might want to refer to the Coaching Drills for Simple Secret #6 for advice on the number of words on a slide. But Taylor makes a good point. Keeping the words to a minimum will help make your presentations that much sharper. Remember, there are plenty of visual techniques, other than text, to make your slides come alive.

Too many statistics will also kill the presentation. Use statistics sparingly. Save the bulk of your numbers for the hand-outs at the end of the presentation. There are also ways of making statistics more visually appealing by using graphics to tell your story. There are several good books and resources on this subject which I've added to the Coaching Drills of this chapter.

Too much parroting: Most presenters read their slides. Great communicators don't. Remember our conversation about Cisco's John Chambers? He has the content of each slide memorized. All he does is glance at the slide once, then speaks to the audience for the rest of the discussion. It's the simplest thing you can do to stand apart as a PPT presenter. But even the great corporate speakers have had to learn this concept. Cisco CEO

John Chambers wasn't born with a PPT clicker in his hand. He's evolved over the past eight years according to Cisco vice president Ron Ricci. "It's easy to get addicted and dependent on PPT as a mechanism for organizing your thinking," says Ricci. "John has evolved into a much richer, deeper presenter. He's figured out how to be himself and work the room. He's gone from reading slides to internalizing the content so he can move off the stage and literally break through the barrier that separates the speaker from the audience.

Showing a command of PPT is critical to evolving as a great business presenter. I was shocked one day when I saw Governor Arnold Schwarzenegger use a PPT show to propose a $15 billion California bond. He also uses PPT for his budget presentations. He loves it and does a masterful job of using the slides to compliment his message. I was shocked because I rarely see political leaders use PPT. But Schwarzenegger is a twenty-first-century speaker, constantly seeking to grow and reinvent himself.

Men's Wearhouse CEO George Zimmer keeps his brand fresh by seeking insight from nontraditional thinkers. In June 2004, the company nominated spiritual guru Deepak Chopra to sit on its board. The Indian-born doctor turned new age master isn't exactly the kind of person you'd associate with a men's apparel chain, but according to Zimmer, he's a "new paradigm" business thinker. In an interview for the *San Francisco Chronicle,* Zimmer said, "In the old business paradigm, there is only one stakeholder, the shareholder. In the new paradigm…there are five stakeholder groups: shareholders, employees, customers, vendors, and the communities in which they do business." A CEO, says Zimmer, has to balance the interest of all five stakeholder groups. It's no wonder Zimmer inspires his employees. He stays contemporary in a traditional industry.

You're Up!

By now I hope you're convinced that making your story interesting, engaging, and visual is critical to winning over your audience and advancing your career. But it's so much more. You might be a scientist working on a cure for cancer, a lab researcher creating material that dissolves in landfills, or an entrepreneur developing a technology that will radically improve our lives. In each situation, effectively pitching and promoting that idea or product is critical to getting it noticed, funded, and created! The world needs you. Your message is important. But nobody will hear you unless you identify and adopt the 10 Simple Secrets.

Build rapport with your audience by being passionate, inspirational, and prepared for your presentation. Craft your message by starting strong, making it clear, and keeping it brief. Get your audience to act on your message by packaging yourself as a leader with the way you talk, walk, and look. If you don't someone else will.

Now that we've come to the conclusion of this chapter, I've got to let you in on another secret. You see, like any good story—and good communicators are good storytellers—this one, too, has a twist. It's like the movie *The Sixth Sense;* just when you think it's over, there's more. I'll level with you. There aren't really 10 Simple Secrets—there are 11!

1. **Reinvent Yourself.** What contemporary references can you include in your next presentation? Think about popular movies, events, or music. When is the last time you shared new management strategies, insights, or book recommendations with your colleagues, customers, or employees? What can you share with them to improve the way they do business? Do you read the same newspapers and magazines every week? If so, break out of the mold and read something completely out of character. You'll be surprised at how much fresh material you'll be able to incorporate into your speeches, pitches, and presentations by climbing out of your shell.

2. **PowerPoint References.** You owe it to yourself and your listeners to not only learn PPT but to deliver your presentations effectively. If you would like to learn more about creating and delivering powerful PPT presentations, Microsoft maintains an extensive website with training, tutorials, and advice at www.microsoft.com/powerpoint.

There are thousands of books on the subject as well. An Amazon.com search will turn up more than four thousand results. Sorry, I haven't read all of them. But I especially like *Using Microsoft Office PowerPoint* by Que Publishing. Be warned—it's a monster at 745 pages. It's billed as "the only PowerPoint book you need." It covers everything. It might be more than you need, but I was struck by the fact that 15 percent of the pages are devoted not to creating slides but to delivering the presentations. It covers everything from where to place people in a room to where to stand when you're in front of them.

If a 745-page guide seems a bit intimidating, the *Dummies* series is usually pretty good. *PowerPoint for Dummies* makes the program very easy to understand. The authors have mastered Simple Secret #5, clarity. The *Dummies* series has been a monstrous mega hit, selling over one hundred million copies. The formula works because readers crave information delivered in terms and language they can easily understand.

Even if you have someone else create the slides for you, you'll never be considered a great communicator if you can't deliver those slides persuasively. A thorough knowledge of the program can help.

SIMPLE SECRET #11: BELIEVE YOU BELONG

"Believe, deep down in your heart, that you're destined to do great things."

JOE PATERNO

None of the secrets revealed in the last ten chapters will do anything to improve your skill as a communicator in your personal or professional life unless you believe you belong in the same category as the men and women interviewed and profiled in this book. Maya Angelou once said, "A solitary fantasy can transform one million realities." But not if you can't articulate it! The key to transforming one million realities is to begin by changing your own. How you think about your role as a spokesperson for your service, product, company, or cause will have an enormous impact on your success. You may believe deeply in your message but you've got to believe in your ability to deliver it.

I once worked with a woman who knew more about a particular government program than anyone on the staff. This particular program helped thousands of people improve their living conditions, but there were many who didn't know about it. Her superiors called me in to help her develop a more effective presentation style. The woman was absolutely terrified of speaking in public. In fact, she didn't want a videocamera to be in the room nor did she ever want photographs taken of herself. The woman had a lifelong fear of speaking after her parents and teachers verbally demeaned her, beginning at a young age. Her transformation had to start in her own head, with her own self talk.

I began by getting this particular client to tell me about the program she administers.

"Sounds like you know a lot about the program," I said.

"Yes, I do," she said bashfully.

"Does anyone in the office know as much as you do?"

"No, they don't."

"Does anyone in the district, county, or state know as much as you do?"

"Actually, no."

"So, you're the expert!" I exclaimed.

"Yes, I guess you can say I am," she responded.

"So why are you keeping this material to yourself? Shouldn't you share this information with others? You said yourself most people don't know these programs exist."

"I guess so. I never really thought of myself as someone people would want to listen to," she acknowledged.

And so we began. No video, no slides, no formal presentation. We started by changing the words this woman used to describe herself, her self-talk. In this book, we've spent so much time talking about what to say to others when what you say to yourself counts just as much.

What do you say to yourself when you're presenting? Do you tell yourself that you have an exciting message that will change the lives of the people in your audience or do you knock yourself down by saying nobody's interested in your subject and in you as a speaker? If you hope to win over your audience, you've got to think like great communicators. Remember when Schwarzenegger's advisor said "Arnold is incapable of seeing the down side of things"? His presentations reflect that positive approach to life. He has fun and it shows. He believes in his message and in himself. As a result, when he speaks, Schwarzenegger is happy and engaging, radiating energy and enthusiasm. Most people can't help but like him. The same was said of Ronald Reagan. Reagan believed in his message and in his ability to persuade others to believe it as well.

★ ★ ★

If you're the head of a company, a division, or a group, you owe it to your team to be the person they look to for motivation. *Dilbert* creator

Scott Adams told me, "I think bringing in the motivational speaker is a sure sign you've given up. It's raising the white flag. If you bring in the humor consultant and the motivational speaker, you have no idea how to inspire your team." I agree. This year a motivational conference came through my town; a high energy talk-fest intended to motivate salespeople to get off their rears, I guess. One reporter who covered it for the *San Jose Mercury News* said he was motivated...to leave! You see, here's the dirty little secret behind most "motivational" speakers—in my opinion, they speak to sell books and they sell books to sell seminars. They offer little, if any, new insights in either one of them. But bosses continue to believe these speakers will motivate their employees to sell more products and get more customers. One woman at this particular show said she attended because her boss was going to quiz her about it the next day. What do you think Adams would have to say about that guy? Don't look to outsiders to inspire your team. Look to yourself.

Someday You'll Pay to Hear Me Sing

Toby Keith is one of the hottest acts in country music. If you like country, you've probably heard of him. If not, perhaps you heard about the controversy he generated when Peter Jennings refused to allow Keith to sing his popular song, "The Angry American," on an ABC Fourth of July television special. Toby stuck to his guns and didn't do the show, but his album sales soared. This is a man who believes in himself. He had a vision of himself as a successful musician when few people did. Music industry executives at one record label literally shoved Toby out the door and told him that he couldn't write or sing. Toby told a friend of his, "You'll pay to see me sing one day." He created a vision for himself so powerful that nobody could stop it from happening. It was only a matter of time before that vision became a reality. The success of your presentations will be the direct result of the vision you hold of yourself as a speaker.

You're Only as Persuasive as the Pictures You Paint

When Barbara Corcoran started in business, she saw herself as the Queen of New York Real Estate. Corcoran writes, "I pictured myself in great detail, including the clothes I'd wear to address an audience of thousands of people eager to hear my expert advice…my imagination provided a crystal-clear picture of where I wanted to go." Corcoran didn't succeed in speaking to thousands. No, she underestimated herself. Today Corcoran speaks to hundreds of thousands of people on the lecture circuit and as a contributor to the Fox news channel. What picture do you see of yourself? You need to create a vision of yourself as a powerful and persuasive presenter, so charismatic and convincing that your listeners cannot help but believe in your message.

Play the Hand You're Dealt

Sybase CEO John Chen plays tournament bridge. In bridge, he says, "you never complain about the hand you're dealt. Your mission is to make the best out of your cards." Something extraordinary hit me as I was writing about Secret #11. Think about it—nearly every one of the great communicators profiled in this book was dealt what could be perceived as a "bad hand." You'd never have picked them to become the greatest spokespeople in the world. They were either poor, dyslexic, or couldn't speak the language. Some fell flat on their face on their early presentations. But nothing would stop them from fulfilling their destinies. They knew their ability to powerfully communicate their visions would catapult them to the top of their chosen professions.

It's Your Time!

Up until this point, your story has been my passion. It's now time for you to reveal the magnificent message behind your own service, product, company, or cause. It's time for your story to become your passion. It's time to take your rightful place alongside the world's greatest business communicators, winning over your customers, colleagues, peers, and prospects. Who knows, maybe I'll write about you in my next book! You belong. Believe you belong. Remember, once you change the way you see yourself as a speaker, the speaker your audience sees will change.

Now go transform those realities!

ACKNOWLEDGMENTS

I set out to write a book that reveals the simple secrets of great business communicators who inspire everyone in their personal and professional lives. I'm grateful to all those who gave generously of their time to shape this work. You've proven to me, your employees, your customers, and your investors why you hold a rightful place among the world's top business leaders. More than two dozen CEOs, executives, entrepreneurs, and experts offered their time and wisdom. I'd like to thank them all in order of appearance:

Cisco Systems vice president Ron Ricci for sharing his insight into one of the most gifted leaders of the corporate world. Intuit founder Scott Cook for taking the time to meet with me at the gorgeous Intuit campus. His revelations form the foundation for several of the secrets. CEO recruiter James Citrin, who not only added his invaluable insight but introduced me to some of the most impressive leaders I've had the pleasure to meet. Financial advisor Tom Moser, who inspires his colleagues because he lives the 10 Simple Secrets. Author Geoffrey Moore, who is a dream interview for a business journalist. *Dilbert* creator Scott Adams, who reminds me everyday through his work that the lessons and techniques in this book are sorely needed. Starbucks chairman Howard Schultz for taking time out of his busy life to share his passion with us (special thanks to Nancy Kent for being so responsive to my follow-ups). Author Suze Orman for proving that people trust people who speak from the heart. Paul

Wachter, thank you for offering stories about Arnold Schwarzenegger. He has an extraordinary personality and I'm sure is proud to count you as a friend and advisor. Scott Norton, whose energy inspires his clients and whose insights make chapter 9 come alive. Venture capitalist Marty Gagen for inviting me to glimpse a fascinating process rarely seen by outsiders. Former White House chief of staff Leon Panetta for his joy of public service. Reuter's president Devin Wenig for being an authentic leader. Bud Thalman, thank you for sharing your Joe Paterno stories. George Martin for staging an extraordinary annual conference that never fails to inspire. *USA Today* columnist Kevin Maney for helping us understand products that will change our lives. Barbara Corcoran for still believing in the lessons your mom taught you. Commander Matt Eversmann for your service to your country. It's an honor to include a true hero in these pages. Venture capitalist David Moore for teaching us to stay on top of our game. Monster founder Jeff Taylor for proving that business can, and should, be fun. Women for Hire CEO Tory Johnson for creating a powerhouse series of conferences and offering your sensational advice. National Semiconductor CEO Brian Halla for successfully communicating a vision. Sybase CEO John Chen for proving that one need not forget his roots to live the American dream. Author Kevin Ryan for supporting this project and lending your expertise. Patricia Dean for being a truly memorable instructor. Business journalist Stuart Varney for always showing real character and for showing me how to take command of my own career. Dr. David McNeill for never letting us forget that body language speaks volumes. Brenda Connors for your exhaustive research into the communication patterns of great leaders. Men's Wearhouse CEO George Zimmer for being the kind of leader people love to work for. Barneys' Tom Kalenderian for reminding us to dress the part. George De Paris for squeezing me in between appointments with the guy in the White House. Brenda Kinsel for your style and wardrobe advice. And Joe Saul-Sehy for seeing potential hurdles as opportunities.

This book would not have reached the right hands if not for my literary agent, Edward Knappman at New England Publishing Associates. Ed, thanks for seeing the possibility. Ed's office manager, Kristine Schiavi, also deserves kudos for her help in the process.

Ed introduced me to a magnificent partner, my editor at Soucebooks, Hillel Black. Hillel, thank you for sharing my enthusiasm. I could not have asked for a better publisher than Sourcebooks. Everyone has been amazing to work with including Michelle Schoob, Vicky Brown, Allison Thomas, Angie Cimarolli, Todd Stocke, Sarah Tucker, Derek Wegmann, Stephanie Wheatley, and Tom Todd. Dominique, you've assembled an incredible team!

Although too numerous to mention here, I'd like to thank all my dear friends for your supportive thoughts and comments. Special thanks to Ted Allrich, a friend and author who believed in this work from the beginning.

One could not be blessed with a more supportive family. My parents, Francesco and Giuseppina never placed limits on my dreams; Tino, Donna, Fran, and Nick, thanks for all you did and all you continue to do. My in-laws, Ken and Patty Cook, deserve the credit for the author photograph but also for raising the greatest woman I know. Vanessa, you're my angel and my true inspiration.

INDEX

48, 121, 207, 214, 216. *See also* Schultz, Howard

Strock, James 33-34, 44

Sybase 5, 106, 127, 129, 193, 218, 226. *See also* Chen, John

T

Taylor, Jeff 4, 5, 21, 55, 85-87, 206, 217, 218-219. *See also* Monster

Trump, Donald 66, 87, 93-95, 99, 182, 183

Tyco 13, 47

V

Varney, Stuart 70-71, 76, 78, 156-157, 169, 182, 192

Virgin Group 4, 21, 27, 205. *See also* Branson, Richard

W

Wachter, Paul 36, 210. *See also* Schwarzenegger, Arnold

Welch, Jack 10, 21, 22, 32, 42, 44, 105, 110-111, 121, 205. *See also* General Electric

Wenig, Devin 51, 108-109, 115, 215-216. *See also* Reuters

Wind River 111-113

Winfrey, Oprah 23, 31, 33, 67, 85, 90, 96

Women for Hire 95, 164. *See also* Johnson, Tory

Worldcom 13, 47

Y

Yahoo! 153, 180

Z

Zimmer, George 35, 179, 183-185, 186, 187, 220